BILINGUAL BINGO

Jaime A. Lucero

New York • Toronto • London • Auckland • Sydney
Mexico City • New Delhi • Hong Kong • Buenos Aires

Para mi madre—
con mucho cariño y corazón

Cover design by Michelle H. Kim
Interior design by Grafica, Inc.
Interior illustrations by Maxie Chambliss, Anne Kennedy, Brian LaRossa, and Mike Moran

ISBN: 978-0-439-70067-2

9 10   40   21 20 19 18 17 16

Table of Contents

Welcome to *Bilingual Bingo!*

Children of all ages love bingo—there is no doubt about it! Like all bingo games, *Bilingual Bingo* is easy to play and super-fun! But there's an added benefit as well: These reproducible games will help students build fluency and gain confidence as English speakers!

Each bingo game in this book includes 8 different reproducible game boards and a sheet of 20 calling cards. Unlike the traditional bingo board, *Bilingual Bingo* uses a 3 x 3 grid. Every calling card and board has words in English and Spanish, and illustrations to support the words.

How to Play

Before playing, you will need to photocopy and cut apart each board and calling card. Students may enjoy coloring the bingo cards and boards. For added durability, ask students to glue each board and card onto oaktag or cardboard, then laminate them. Use beans or colored chips as tokens. Note: Students can play in groups of eight, or as a whole class using duplicate boards with multiple winners.

Ask students to elect one child to take the role of card caller, or you can have students take turns reading cards. The card caller should shuffle the cards, then place the stack facedown. Next, the caller should take the top card and read the English or Spanish word, or both. Once the card is read, players should look at their boards to see if they have a match. If a match is made, players should place a token on their board. Play continues in this fashion until a player gets three in a row, either vertically, horizontally, or diagonally. Upon achieving three in a row, a child should shout "Bingo!" or "Bilingual Bingo!" The student who shouts out first must then read each English and Spanish word from the winning set. If the child reads all words correctly, he or she wins the game!

Celebrations • Celebraciones

candy	gift	ice cream	balloon
dulce	regalo	helado	globo
cake	cookie	slice	Halloween
pastel	galleta	rebanada	Víspera de Todos los Santos
mask	birthday	card	wedding
máscara	cumpleaños	tarjeta	boda
candle	Christmas tree	New Year	crown
vela	árbol de Navidad	Año Nuevo	corona
fireworks	music	confetti	costume
fuegos artificiales	música	confeti	disfraz

Bilingual Bingo

Celebrations / Celebraciones

balloon / globo	Halloween / Víspera de Todos los Santos	ice cream / helado
New Year / Año Nuevo	costume / disfraz	slice / rebanada
fireworks / fuegos artificiales	music / música	cookie / galleta

Bilingual Bingo

Celebrations / Celebraciones

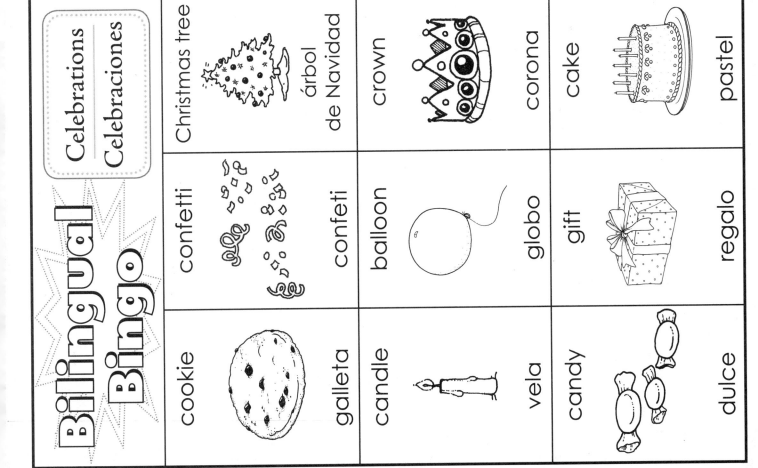

Christmas tree / árbol de Navidad	crown / corona	cake / pastel
confetti / confeti	balloon / globo	gift / regalo
cookie / galleta	candle / vela	candy / dulce

Bilingual Bingo

Celebrations
Celebraciones

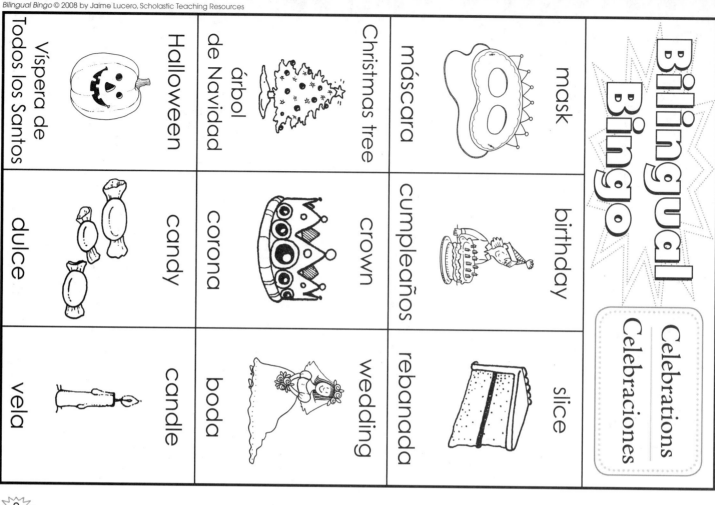

mask / máscara	birthday / cumpleaños	slice / rebanada
Christmas tree / árbol de Navidad	crown / corona	wedding / boda
Halloween / Víspera de Todos los Santos	candy / dulce	candle / vela

Bilingual Bingo

Celebrations
Celebraciones

cake / pastel	card / tarjeta	gift / regalo
crown / corona	slice / rebanada	cookie / galleta
birthday / cumpleaños	New Year / Año Nuevo	mask / máscara

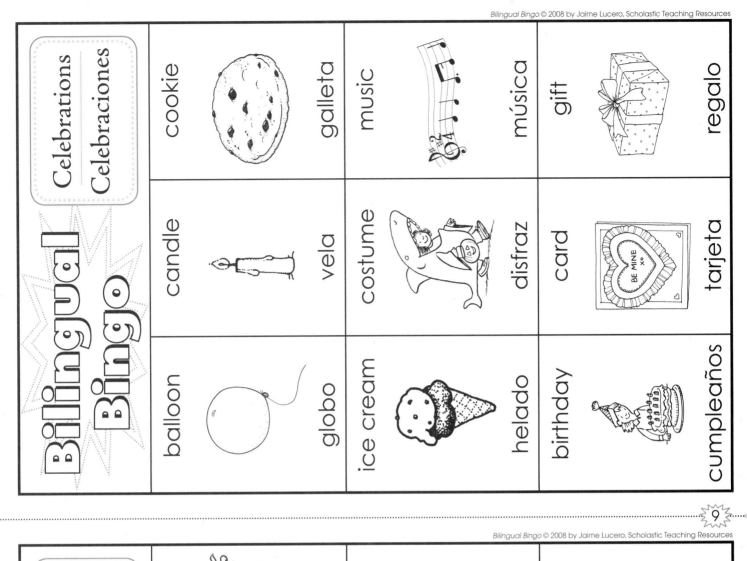

Bilingual Bingo

Celebrations / Celebraciones

cookie / galleta	music / música	gift / regalo
candle / vela	costume / disfraz	card / tarjeta
balloon / globo	ice cream / helado	birthday / cumpleaños

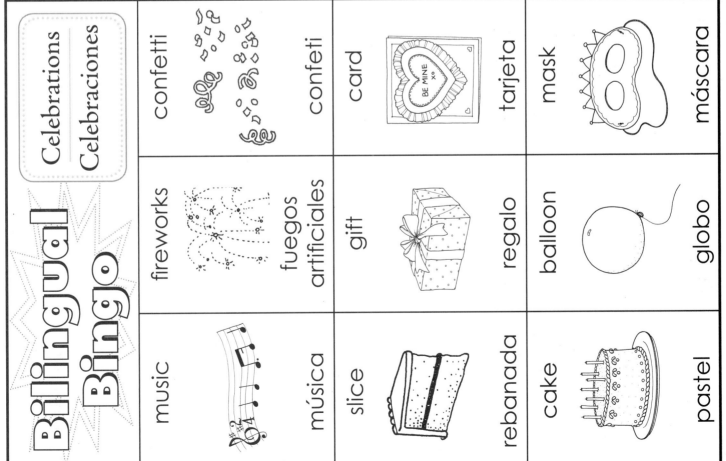

Bilingual Bingo

Celebrations / Celebraciones

confetti / confeti	card / tarjeta	mask / máscara
fireworks / fuegos artificiales	gift / regalo	balloon / globo
music / música	slice / rebanada	cake / pastel

Bilingual Bingo

Celebrations
Celebraciones

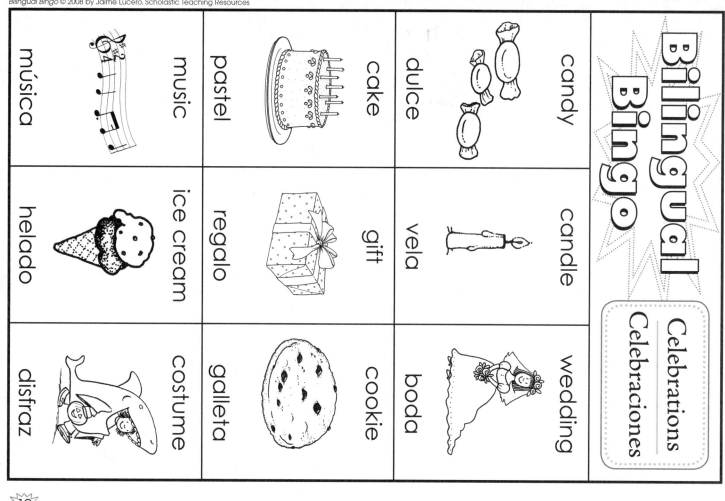

candy	candle	wedding
dulce	vela	boda
		cookie
cake	gift	galleta
pastel	regalo	costume
music	ice cream	disfraz
música	helado	

Bilingual Bingo

Celebrations
Celebraciones

confetti	fireworks	ice cream
confeti	fuegos artificiales	helado
mask	card	gift
máscara	tarjeta	regalo
New Year	Christmas tree	Halloween
Año Nuevo	árbol de Navidad	Víspera de Todos los Santos

hat sombrero	shorts pantalones cortos	t-shirt camiseta	skirt falda
pajama pijama	pant pantalón	slipper pantufla	sock calcetín
blouse blusa	cap gorra	galoshes botas de hule	jacket chaqueta
mitten mitón	shoe zapato	suit traje	tie corbata
dress vestido	sandal sandalia	scarf bufanda	vest chaleco

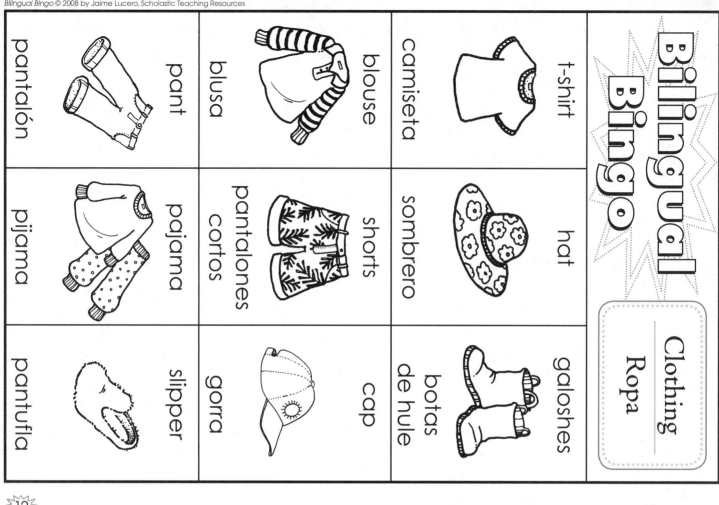

Bilingual Bingo

Clothing
Ropa

t-shirt	hat	galoshes
camiseta	sombrero	botas de hule
blouse	shorts	cap
blusa	pantalones cortos	gorra
pant	pajama	slipper
pantalón	pijama	pantufla

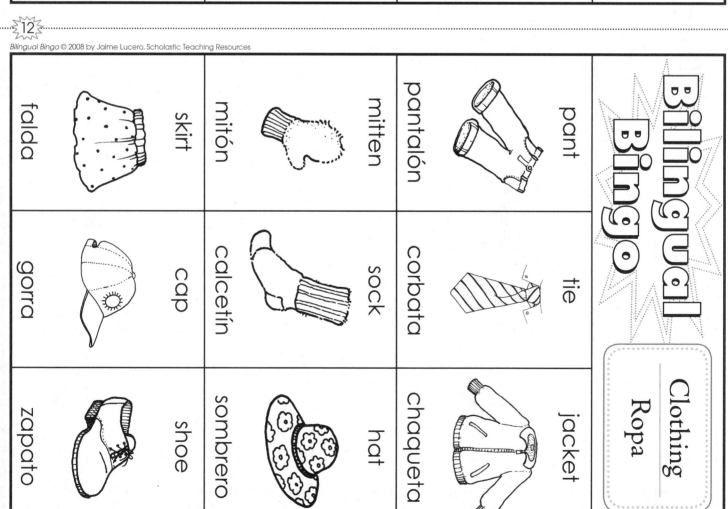

Bilingual Bingo

Clothing
Ropa

pant	tie	jacket
pantalón	corbata	chaqueta
mitten	sock	hat
mitón	calcetín	sombrero
skirt	cap	shoe
falda	gorra	zapato

Bilingual Bingo

Clothing / Ropa

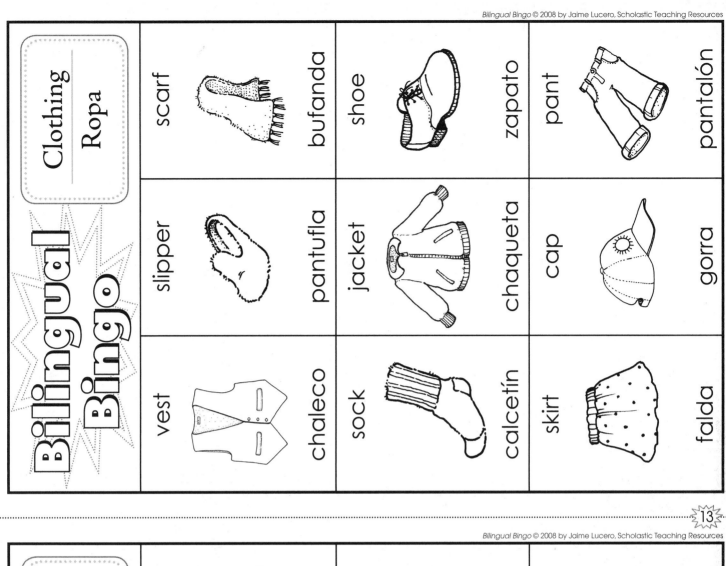

scarf / bufanda	shoe / zapato	pant / pantalón
slipper / pantufla	jacket / chaqueta	cap / gorra
vest / chaleco	sock / calcetín	skirt / falda

Bilingual Bingo

Clothing / Ropa

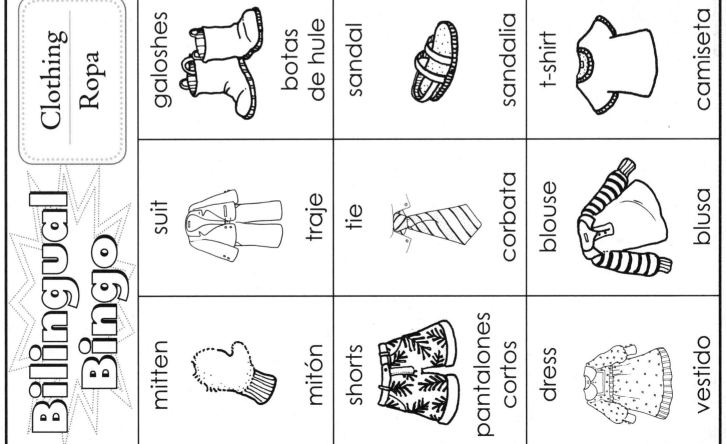

galoshes / botas de hule	sandal / sandalia	t-shirt / camiseta
suit / traje	tie / corbata	blouse / blusa
mitten / mitón	shorts / pantalones cortos	dress / vestido

Bilingual Bingo

Clothing
Ropa

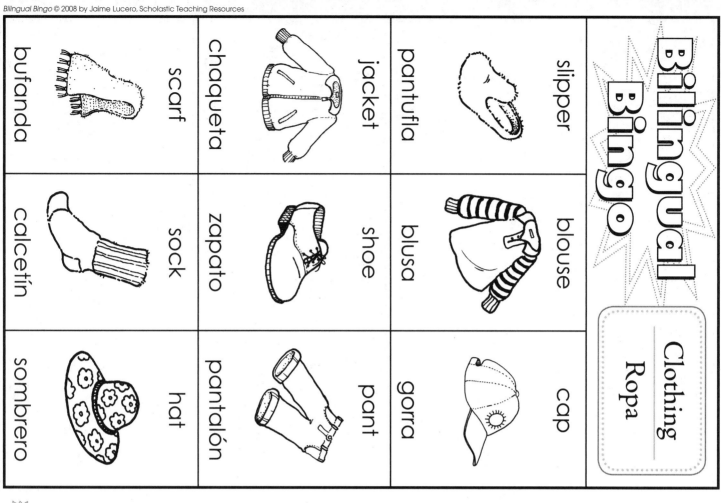

slipper pantufla	jacket chaqueta	scarf bufanda
blouse blusa	shoe zapato	sock calcetín
cap gorra	pant pantalón	hat sombrero

Bilingual Bingo

Clothing
Ropa

suit traje	t-shirt camiseta	galoshes botas de hule
shoe zapato	pajama pijama	sandal sandalia
dress vestido	skirt falda	mitten mitón

Bilingual Bingo

Clothing / Ropa

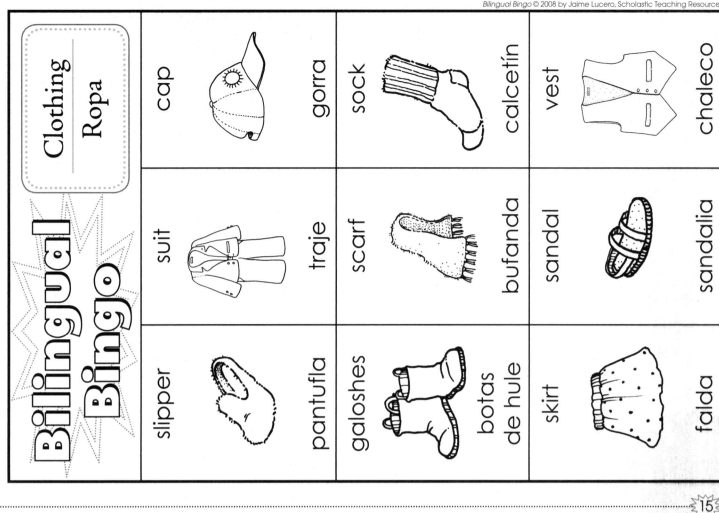

cap — gorra	sock — calcetín	vest — chaleco
suit — traje	scarf — bufanda	sandal — sandalia
slipper — pantufla	galoshes — botas de hule	skirt — falda

Bilingual Bingo

Clothing / Ropa

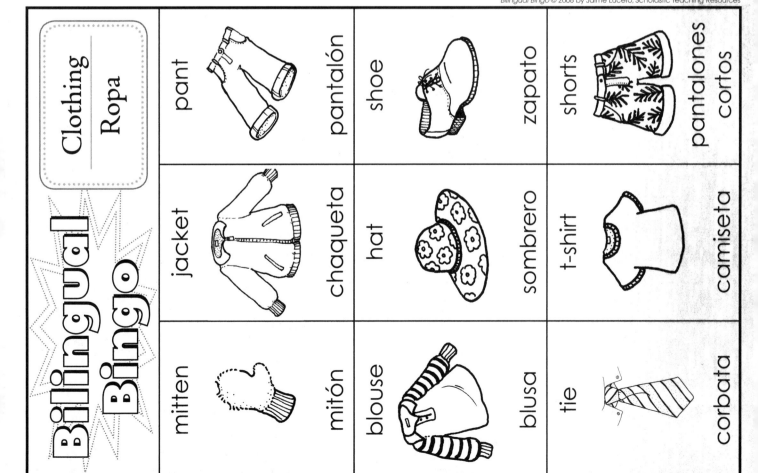

pant — pantalón	shoe — zapato	shorts — pantalones cortos
jacket — chaqueta	hat — sombrero	t-shirt — camiseta
mitten — mitón	blouse — blusa	tie — corbata

The Community • La Comunidad

house casa	fair feria	hospital hospital	marina puerto
school escuela	forest bosque	playground patio de recreo	pool piscina
park parque	zoo zoológico	farm granja	tailor sastre
doctor doctora	baker panadero	nurse enfermera	teacher maestra
firefighter bombero	librarian bibliotecario	police officer agente de policía	veterinarian veterinaria

Bilingual Bingo

The Community
La Comunidad

playground

patio de recreo

park

parque

fair

feria

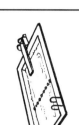

pool

piscina

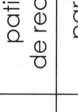

teacher

maestra

tailor

sastre

nurse

enfermera

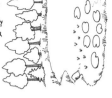

school

escuela

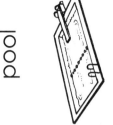

police officer

agente de policía

Bilingual Bingo

The Community
La Comunidad

librarian

bibliotecario

hospital

hospital

baker

panadero

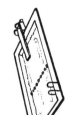

zoo

zoológico

farm

granja

doctor

doctora

firefighter

bombero

veterinarian

veterinaria

house

casa

Bilingual Bingo © 2008 by Jaime Lucero, Scholastic Teaching Resources

18

Bilingual Bingo

The Community
La Comunidad

police officer / agente de policía	doctor / doctora	school / escuela
zoo / zoológico	pool / piscina	house / casa
veterinarian / veterinaria	teacher / maestra	hospital / hospital

Bilingual Bingo

The Community
La Comunidad

veterinarian / veterinaria	tailor / sastre	farm / granja
park / parque	baker / panadero	playground / patio de recreo
nurse / enfermera	marina / puerto	pool / piscina

Bilingual Bingo

pool / piscina	teacher / maestra	farm / granja
park / parque	tailor / sastre	house / casa
playground / patio de recreo	school / escuela	tailor / bibliotecario

---

Bilingual Bingo

firefighter / bombero	zoo / zoológico	forest / bosque
baker / panadero	nurse / enfermera	doctor / doctora
marina / puerto	hospital / hospital	fair / feria

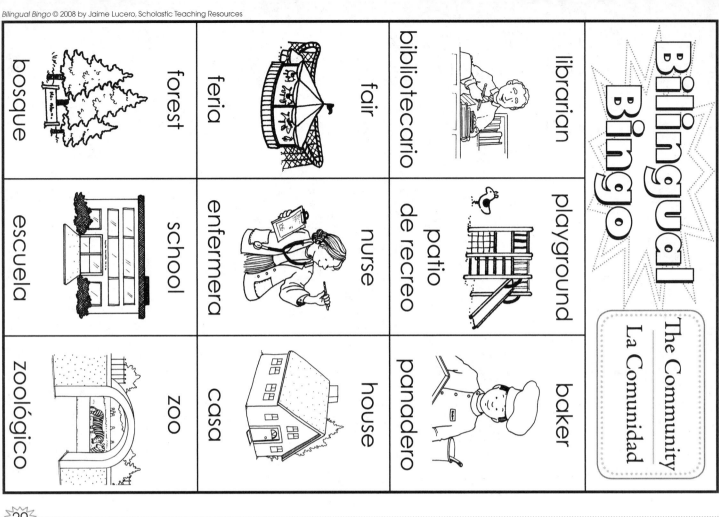

Bilingual Bingo

The Community
La Comunidad

librarian	playground	baker
bibliotecario	patio de recreo	panadero
fair	nurse	house
feria	enfermera	casa
forest	school	zoo
bosque	escuela	zoológico

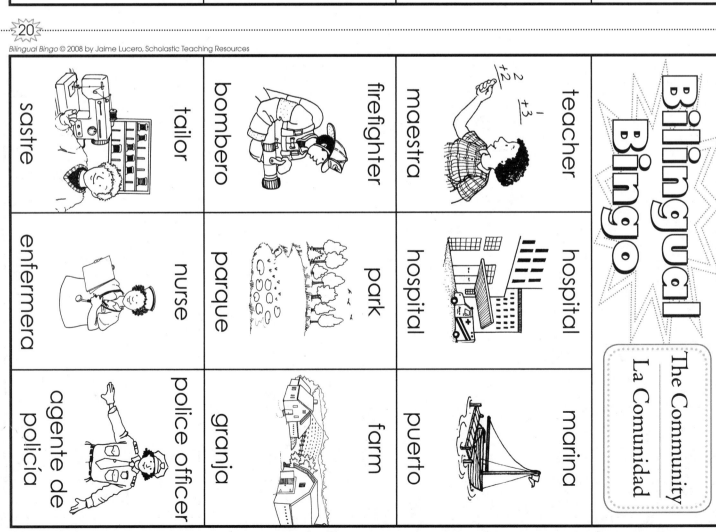

Bilingual Bingo

The Community
La Comunidad

teacher	hospital	marina
maestra	hospital	puerto
firefighter	park	farm
bombero	parque	granja
tailor	nurse	police officer
sastre	enfermera	agente de policía

Farm Animals • Animales de la Granja

cat gato	dog perro	cow vaca	mouse ratón
pig cerdo	chick pollito	lamb cordero	rabbit conejo
hen gallina	horse caballo	turkey guajolote	duck pato
frog rana	rooster gallo	goose ganso	mule mula
goat cabra	bird pájaro	snail caracol	owl búho

Bilingual Bingo

Farm Animals
Animales de la Granja

hen / gallina	pig / cerdo	frog / rana
cat / gato	goat / cabra	bird / pájaro
dog / perro	rooster / gallo	horse / caballo

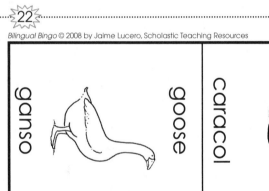

Bilingual Bingo

Farm Animals
Animales de la Granja

chick / pollito	snail / caracol	goose / ganso
cow / vaca	lamb / cordero	turkey / guajolote
owl / búho	mouse / ratón	rabbit / conejo

Bilingual Bingo

Farm Animals
Animales de la Granja

dog / perro 	cat / gato	rabbit / conejo
horse / caballo	mouse / ratón	snail / caracol
owl / búho	cow / vaca	lamb / cordero

Bilingual Bingo

Farm Animals
Animales de la Granja

rooster / gallo	mule / mula	bird / pájaro
pig / cerdo	chick / pollito	turkey / guajolote
duck / pato	frog / rana	hen / gallina

Bilingual Bingo

Farm Animals
Animales de la Granja

bird / pájaro	mouse / ratón	horse / caballo
duck / pato	frog / rana	cat / gato
goose / ganso	hen / gallina	chick / pollito

Bilingual Bingo

Farm Animals
Animales de la Granja

goat / cabra	snail / caracol	rabbit / conejo
dog / perro	lamb / cordero	owl / búho
pig / cerdo	mule / mula	turkey / guajolote

Bilingual Bingo

Farm Animals
Animales de la Granja

snail / caracol	duck / pato	mule / mula
cat / gato	mouse / ratón	owl / búho
horse / caballo	rabbit / conejo	goose / ganso

Bilingual Bingo

Farm Animals
Animales de la Granja

goat / cabra	dog / perro	cow / vaca
chick / pollito	pig / cerdo	frog / rana
rooster / gallo	hen / gallina	bird / pájaro

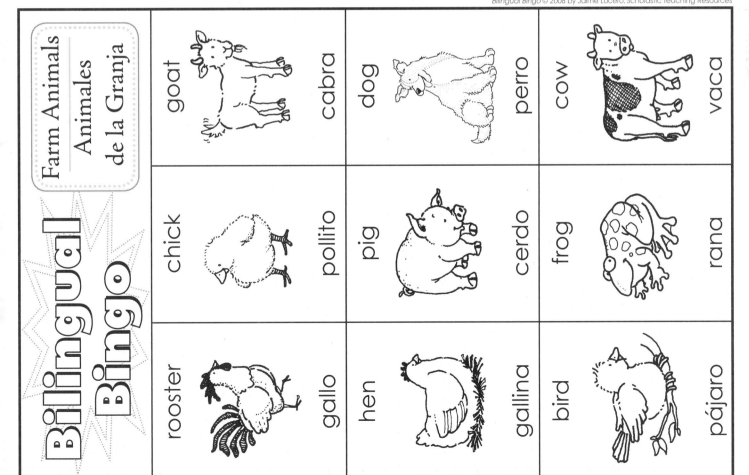

Fruits and Vegetables • Frutas y Verduras

apple	strawberry	lemon	peach
manzana	fresa	limón	durazno
banana	cherries	grapes	orange
plátano	cerezas	uvas	naranja
pear	coconut	melon	pineapple
pera	coco	melón	piña
watermelon	carrot	tomato	corn
sandía	zanahoria	tomate	elote
cucumber	celery	peas	pumpkin
pepino	apio	guisantes	calabaza

Bilingual Bingo

Fruits and Vegetables
Frutas y Verduras

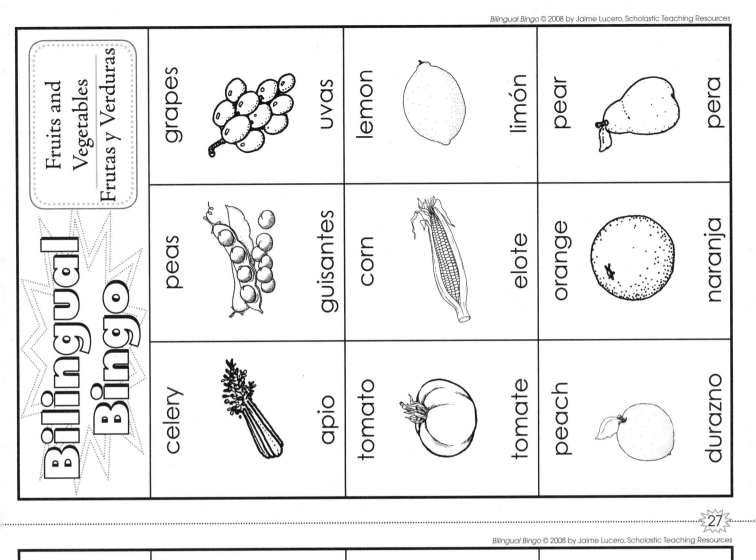

grapes / uvas
lemon / limón
pear / pera
peas / guisantes
corn / elote
orange / naranja
celery / apio
tomato / tomate
peach / durazno

27

Bilingual Bingo

Fruits and Vegetables
Frutas y Verduras

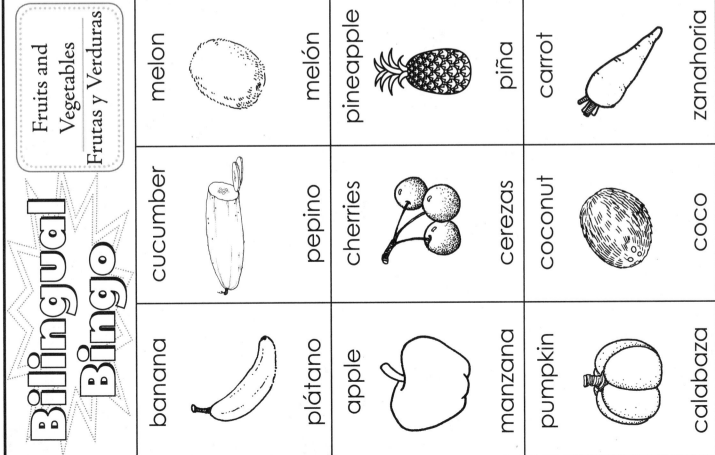

melon / melón
pineapple / piña
carrot / zanahoria
cucumber / pepino
cherries / cerezas
coconut / coco
banana / plátano
apple / manzana
pumpkin / calabaza

Bilingual Bingo

Fruits and
Vegetables
Frutas y Verduras

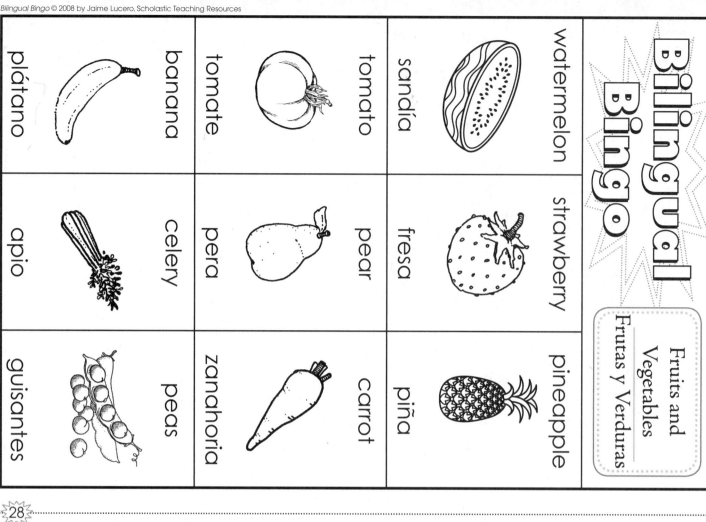

watermelon / sandía	strawberry / fresa	pineapple / piña
tomato / tomate	pear / pera	carrot / zanahoria
banana / plátano	celery / apio	peas / guisantes

Bilingual Bingo

Fruits and
Vegetables
Frutas y Verduras

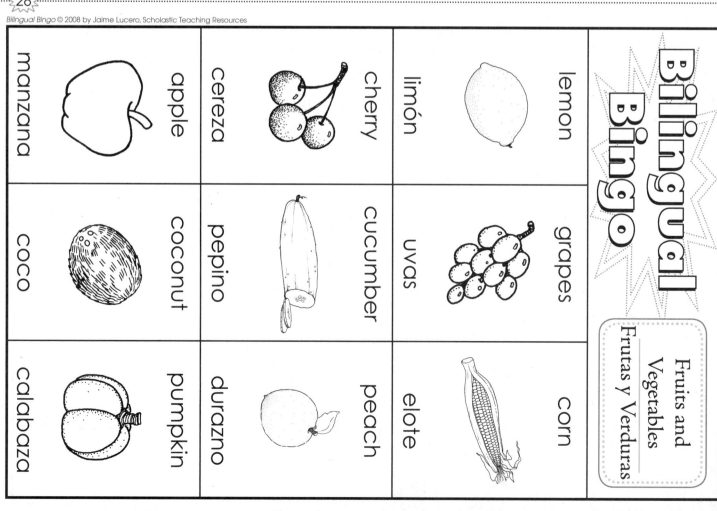

lemon / limón	grapes / uvas	corn / elote
cherry / cereza	cucumber / pepino	peach / durazno
apple / manzana	coconut / coco	pumpkin / calabaza

Bilingual Bingo

Fruits and Vegetables
Frutas y Verduras

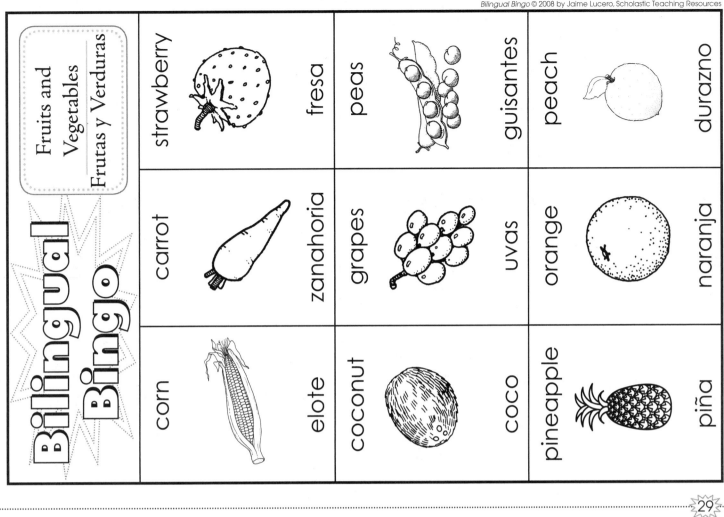

strawberry / fresa	peas / guisantes	peach / durazno
carrot / zanahoria	grapes / uvas	orange / naranja
corn / elote	coconut / coco	pineapple / piña

Bilingual Bingo

Fruits and Vegetables
Frutas y Verduras

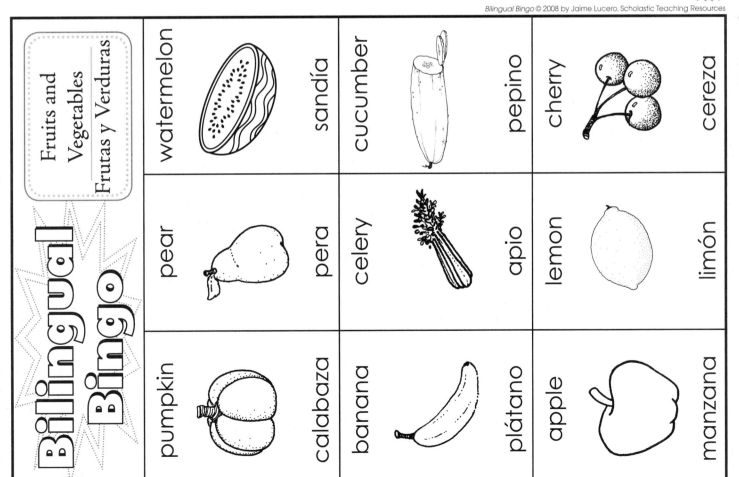

watermelon / sandía	cucumber / pepino	cherry / cereza
pear / pera	celery / apio	lemon / limón
pumpkin / calabaza	banana / plátano	apple / manzana

Bilingual Bingo

Fruits and Vegetables
Frutas y Verduras

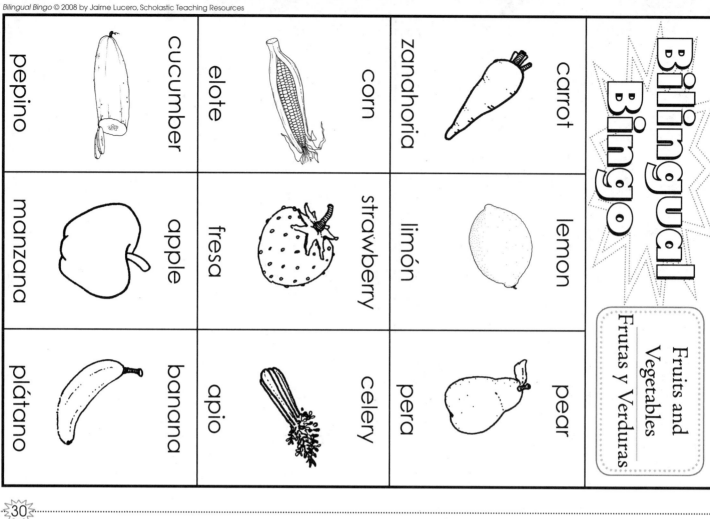

carrot / zanahoria	lemon / limón	pear / pera
corn / elote	strawberry / fresa	celery / apio
cucumber / pepino	apple / manzana	banana / plátano

Bilingual Bingo

Fruits and Vegetables
Frutas y Verduras

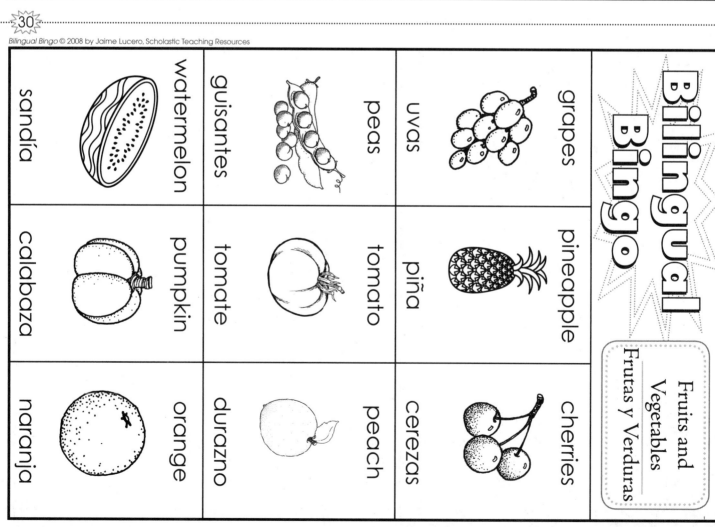

grapes / uvas	pineapple / piña	cherries / cerezas
peas / guisantes	tomato / tomate	peach / durazno
watermelon / sandía	pumpkin / calabaza	orange / naranja

telephone	cup	pitcher	stove
teléfono	taza	jarra	estufa

door	pillow	tooth brush	spoon
puerta	almohada	cepillo de dientes	cuchara

bed	glass	plate	fan
cama	vaso	plato	abanico

key	ladder	lamp	newspaper
llave	escalera	lámpara	periódico

sink	table	window	pail
fregadero	mesa	ventana	balde

Bilingual Bingo

In My House
En Mi Casa

bed	telephone	key
cama	teléfono	llave
glass	window	plate
vaso	ventana	plato
pillow	door	ladder
almohada	puerta	escalera

Bilingual Bingo

In My House
En Mi Casa

lamp	table	stove
lámpara	mesa	estufa
cup	toothbrush	pail
taza	cepillo de dientes	balde
pitcher	spoon	newspaper
jarra	cuchara	periódico

Bilingual Bingo

In My House / En Mi Casa

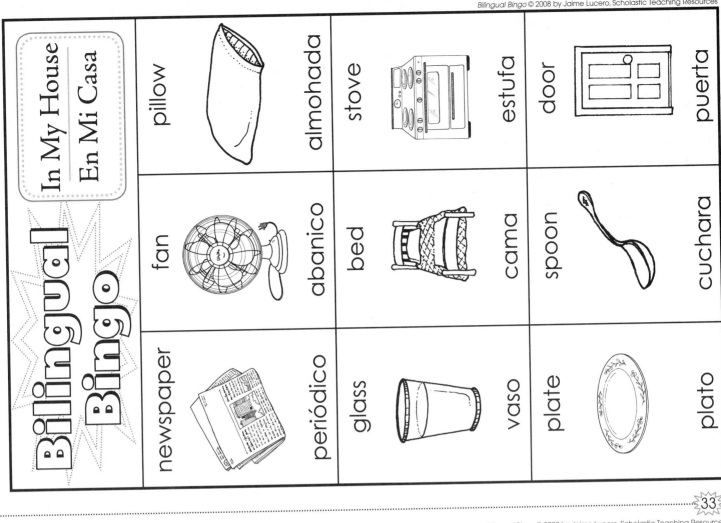

pillow / almohada	stove / estufa	door / puerta
fan / abanico	bed / cama	spoon / cuchara
newspaper / periódico	glass / vaso	plate / plato

Bilingual Bingo

In My House / En Mi Casa

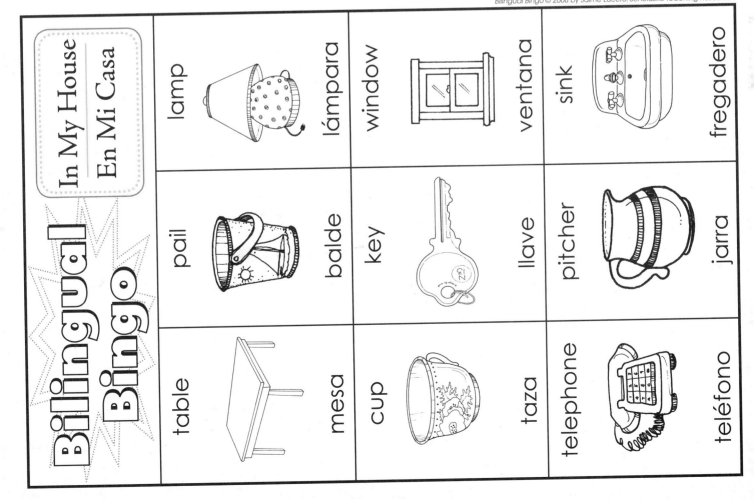

lamp / lámpara	window / ventana	sink / fregadero
pail / balde	key / llave	pitcher / jarra
table / mesa	cup / taza	telephone / teléfono

Bilingual Bingo

In My House
En Mi Casa

newspaper / periódico	spoon / cuchara	glass / vaso
door / puerta	table / mesa	cup / taza
key / llave	toothbrush / cepillo de dientes	window / ventana

Bilingual Bingo

In My House
En Mi Casa

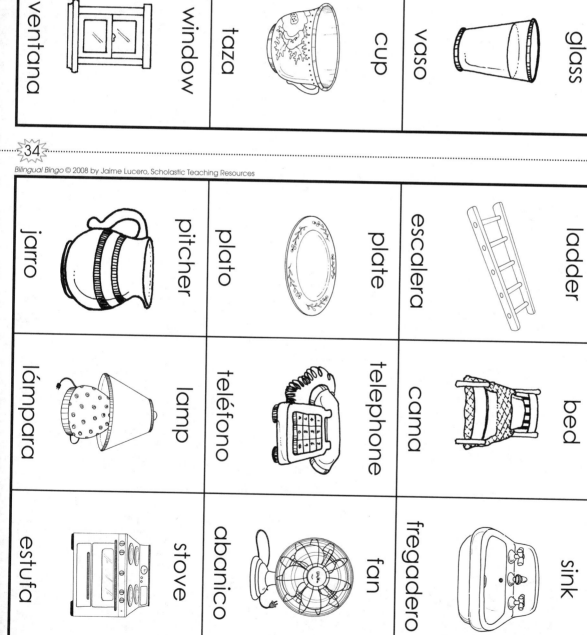

ladder / escalera	bed / cama	sink / fregadero
plate / plato	telephone / teléfono	fan / abanico
pitcher / jarro	lamp / lámpara	stove / estufa

Bilingual Bingo

In My House / En Mi Casa

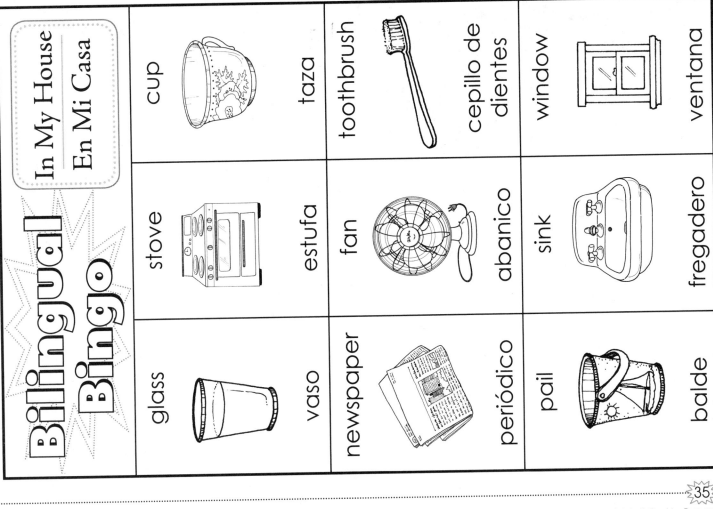

cup	toothbrush	window
taza	cepillo de dientes	ventana
stove	fan	sink
estufa	abanico	fregadero
glass	newspaper	pail
vaso	periódico	balde

Bilingual Bingo

In My House / En Mi Casa

bed	table	lamp
cama	mesa	lámpara
pillow	ladder	door
almohada	escalera	puerta
plate	key	telephone
plato	llave	teléfono

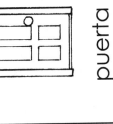
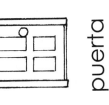

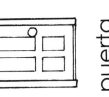
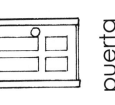
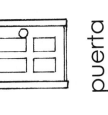

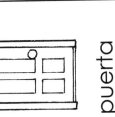

Insects (and Other Bugs) • Insectos (y Otros Bichos)

mosquito	butterfly	dragonfly	beetle
mosquito	mariposa	libélula	escarabajo
ant	bee	praying mantis	cockroach
hormiga	abeja	mantis religiosa	cucaracha
moth	fly	cricket	flea
polilla	mosca	grillo	pulga
weevil	ladybug	firefly	cicada
gorgojo	mariquita	luciérnaga	chicharra
caterpillar	spider	earthworm	centipede
oruga	araña	gusano	ciempiés

Bilingual Bingo

Insects
and Other Bugs
Insectos
y Otros Bichos

cicada / chicharra	mosquito / mosquito	cricket / grillo
weevil / gorgojo	beetle / escarabajo	spider / araña
caterpillar / oruga	butterfly / mariposa	centipede / ciempiés

37

Bilingual Bingo

Insects
and Other Bugs
Insectos
y Otros Bichos

earthworm / gusano	bee / abeja	cockroach / cucaracha
fly / mosca	flea / pulga	moth / polilla
dragonfly / libélula	ladybug / mariquita	firefly / luciérnaga

Bilingual Bingo

cricket 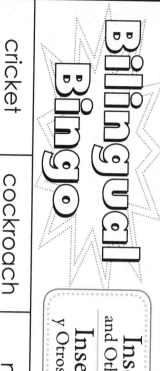	cockroach 	moth 
grilo	cucaracha	polilla
beetle 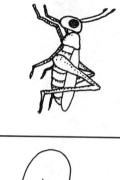	praying mantis 	bee
escarabajo	mantis religiosa	abeja
centipede	ladybug	cicada
ciempiés	mariquita	chicharra

Bilingual Bingo

ant 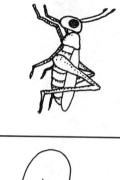	butterfly	flea 
hormiga	mariposa	pulga
fly 	dragonfly 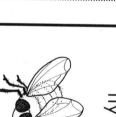	spider 
mosca	libélula	araña
caterpillar 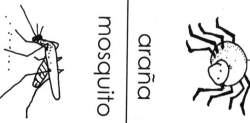	earthworm 	mosquito 
oruga	gusano	mosquito

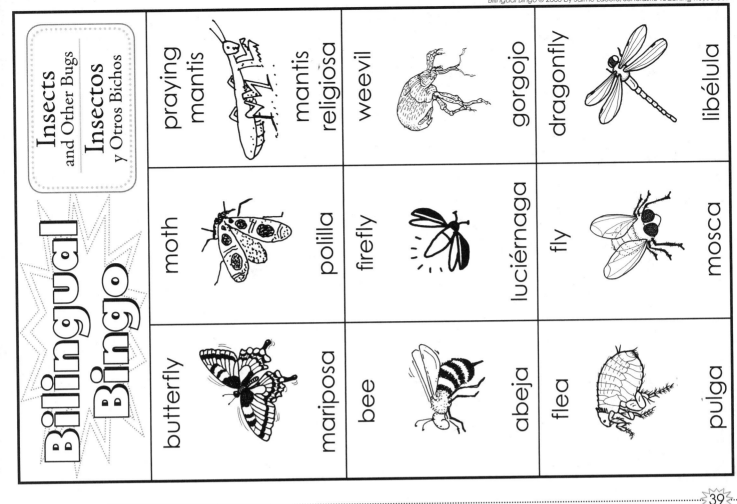

Bilingual Bingo

Insects and Other Bugs
Insectos y Otros Bichos

praying mantis / mantis religiosa	weevil / gorgojo	dragonfly / libélula
moth / polilla	firefly / luciérnaga	fly / mosca
butterfly / mariposa	bee / abeja	flea / pulga

39

Bilingual Bingo

Insects and Other Bugs
Insectos y Otros Bichos

ant / hormiga	cricket / grillo	centipede / ciempiés
spider / araña	earthworm / gusano	beetle / escarabajo
caterpillar / oruga	mosquito / mosquito	ladybug / mariquita

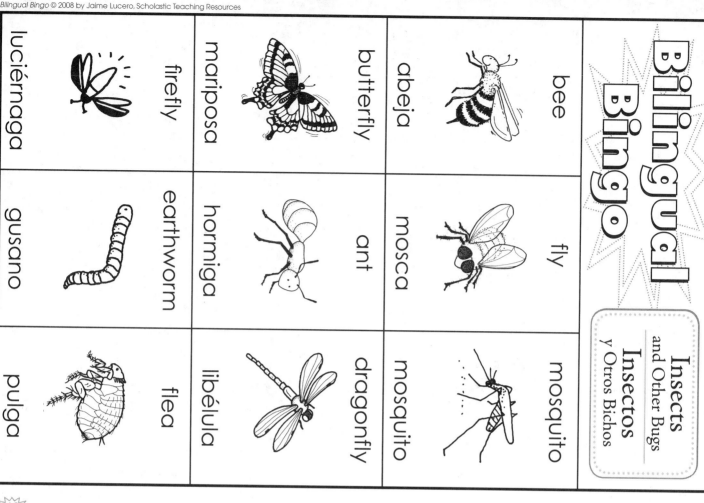

Bilingual Bingo

Insects and Other Bugs
Insectos y Otros Bichos

bee	fly	mosquito
abeja	mosca	mosquito
butterfly	ant	dragonfly
mariposa	hormiga	libélula
firefly	earthworm	flea
luciérnaga	gusano	pulga

Bilingual Bingo

Insects and Other Bugs
Insectos y Otros Bichos

cricket	ladybug	centipede
grillo	mariquita	ciempiés
mantis religiosa	caterpillar	beetle
mantis religiosa	oruga	escarabajo
moth	weevil	cockroach
polilla	gorgojo	cucaracha

Let's Eat • Vamos a Comer

cereal	hamburger	bread	soup
cereal	hamburguesa	pan	sopa
cheese	noodles	hot dog	turkey
queso	tallarínes	perro caliente	pavo
fried egg	pie	milk	steak
huevo frito	pastel con fruta	leche	bistec
juice	jam	spaghetti	sandwich
jugo	mermelada	espagueti	emparedado
breakfast	lunch	rice	salad
desayuno	almuerzo	arroz	ensalada

Bilingual Bingo

Let's Eat
Vamos a Comer

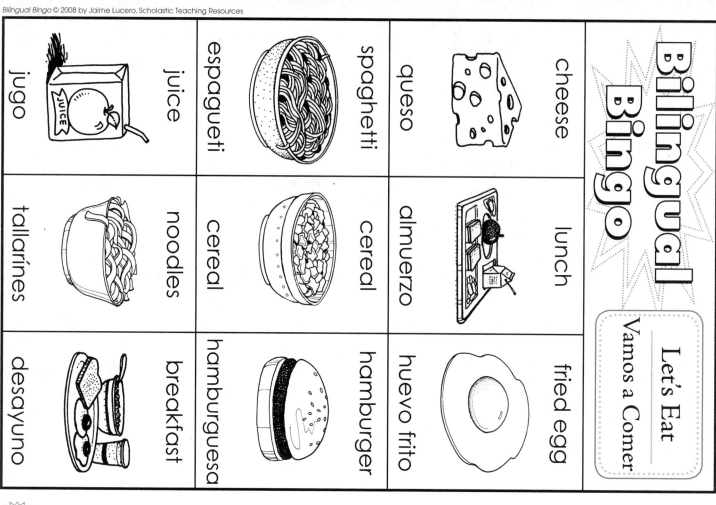

cheese / queso	lunch / almuerzo	fried egg / huevo frito
spaghetti / espagueti	cereal / cereal	hamburger / hamburguesa
juice / jugo	noodles / tallarínes	breakfast / desayuno

Bilingual Bingo

Let's Eat
Vamos a Comer

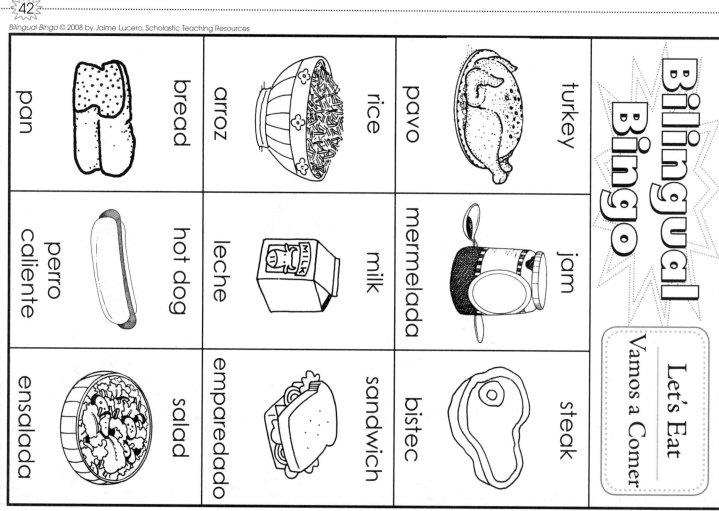

turkey / pavo	jam / mermelada	steak / bistec
rice / arroz	milk / leche	sandwich / emparedado
bread / pan	hot dog / perro caliente	salad / ensalada

Bilingual Bingo

Let's Eat
Vamos a Comer

lunch — almuerzo	bread — pan	milk — leche
pie — pastel con fruta	rice — arroz	cereal — cereal
steak — bistec	sandwich — emparedado	salad — ensalada

Bilingual Bingo

Let's Eat
Vamos a Comer

spaghetti — espagueti	soup — sopa	breakfast — desayuno
hot dog — perro caliente	cheese — queso	turkey — pavo
juice — jugo	fried egg — huevo frito	hamburger — hamburguesa

Bilingual Bingo

Let's Eat
Vamos a Comer

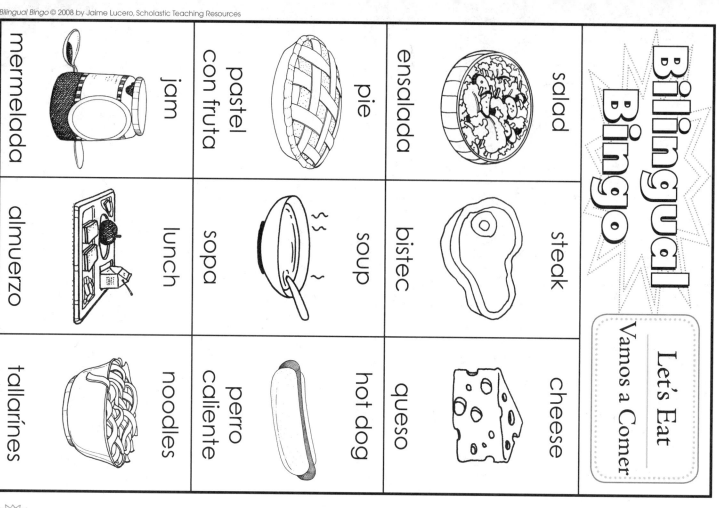

salad / ensalada	steak / bistec	cheese / queso
pie / pastel con fruta	soup / sopa	hot dog / perro caliente
jam / mermelada	lunch / almuerzo	noodles / tallarínes

Bilingual Bingo

Let's Eat
Vamos a Comer

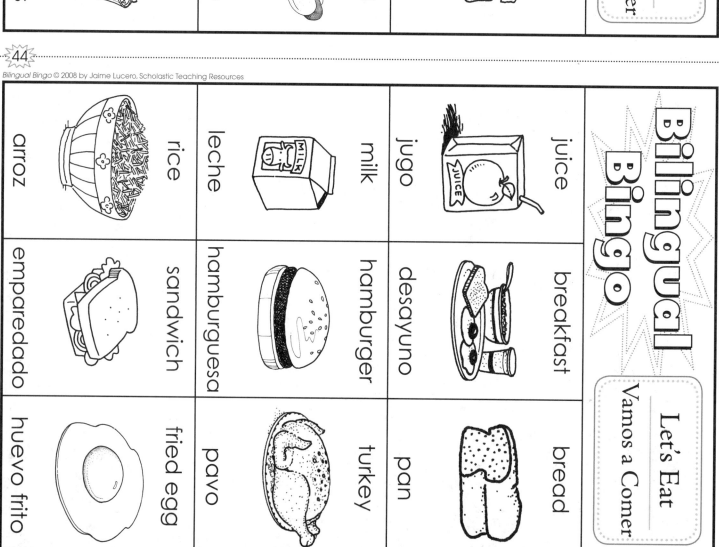

juice / jugo	breakfast / desayuno	bread / pan
milk / leche	hamburger / hamburguesa	turkey / pavo
rice / arroz	sandwich / emparedado	fried egg / huevo frito

Bilingual Bingo

Let's Eat
Vamos a Comer

breakfast / desayuno	cheese / queso	lunch / almuerzo
salad / ensalada	pie / pastel con fruta	cereal / cereal
jam / mermelada	rice / arroz	milk / leche

Bilingual Bingo

Let's Eat
Vamos a Comer

turkey / pavo	juice / jugo	steak / bistec
fried egg / huevo frito	bread / pan	noodles / tallarines
sandwich / emparedado	hamburger / hamburguesa	soup / sopa

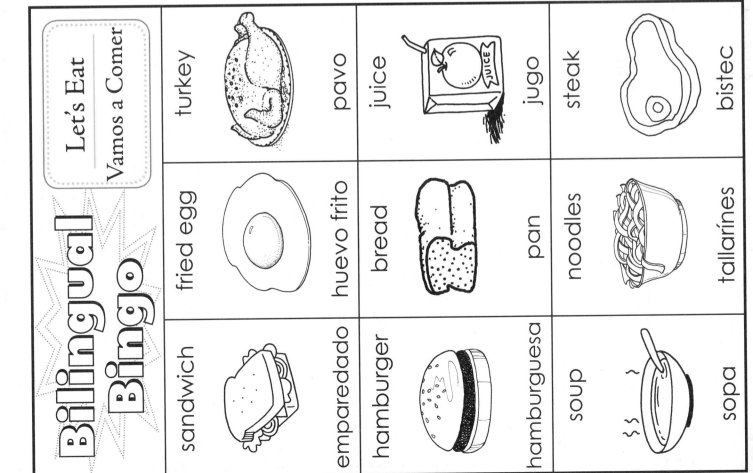

Math • Matemáticas

money	penny	dime	nickel
dinero	centavo	diez centavos	cinco centavos

quarter	coins	time	scale
cuarto de dólar	monedas	tiempo	balanza

circle	square	rectangle	triangle
círculo	cuadrado	rectángulo	triángulo

oval	rhombus	cube	cylinder
óvalo	rombo	cubo	cilindro

add	subtract	multiply	divide
$\begin{array}{r}1\\+2\\\hline 3\end{array}$	$\begin{array}{r}5\\-1\\\hline 4\end{array}$	$\begin{array}{r}3\\\times 3\\\hline 9\end{array}$	$2\overline{)6}^{\,3}$
sumar	restar	multiplicar	dividir

Bilingual Bingo

Math / Matemáticas		
triangle triángulo	add $\begin{array}{r} 1 \\ +2 \\ \hline 3 \end{array}$ sumar	circle círculo
dime diez centavos	nickel cinco centavos	time tiempo
square cuadrado	scale balanza	rhombus rombo

Bilingual Bingo

Math / Matemáticas		
rectangle rectángulo	coins monedas	subtract $\begin{array}{r} 5 \\ -1 \\ \hline 4 \end{array}$ restar
penny centavo	oval óvalo	cube cubo
multiply $\begin{array}{r} 3 \\ \times 3 \\ \hline 9 \end{array}$ multiplicar	quarter cuarto de dólar	money dinero

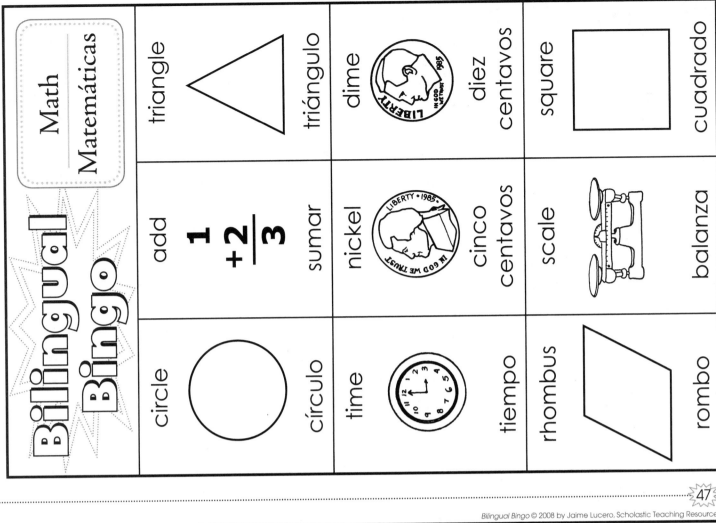

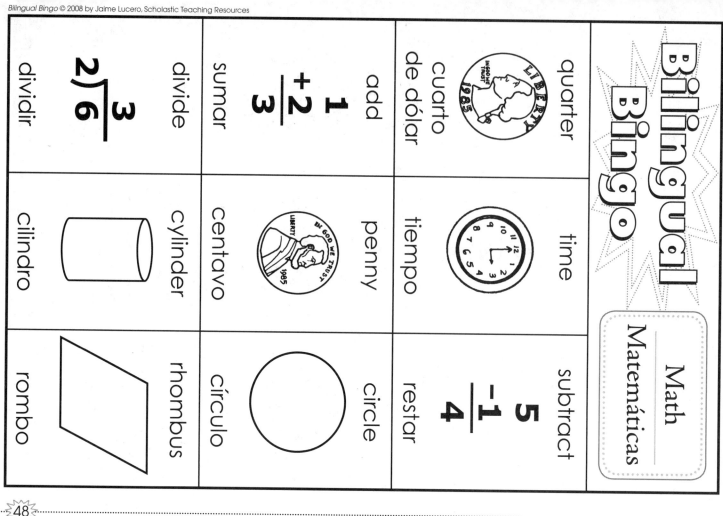

Bilingual Bingo

Math ____
Matemáticas

quarter / cuarto de dólar	time / tiempo	subtract $\begin{array}{r} 5 \\ -1 \\ \hline 4 \end{array}$ / restar
add $\begin{array}{r} 1 \\ +2 \\ \hline 3 \end{array}$ / sumar	penny / centavo	circle / círculo
divide $2\overline{)6}\,3$ / dividir	cylinder / cilindro	rhombus / rombo

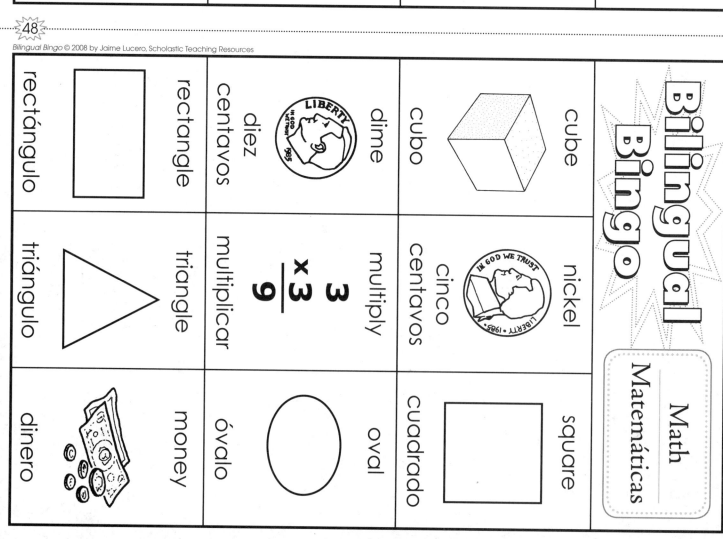

Bilingual Bingo

Math ____
Matemáticas

cube / cubo	dime / diez centavos	rectangle / rectángulo
nickel / cinco centavos	multiply $\begin{array}{r} 3 \\ \times 3 \\ \hline 9 \end{array}$ / multiplicar	triangle / triángulo
square / cuadrado	oval / óvalo	money / dinero

Bilingual Bingo

Math / Matemáticas

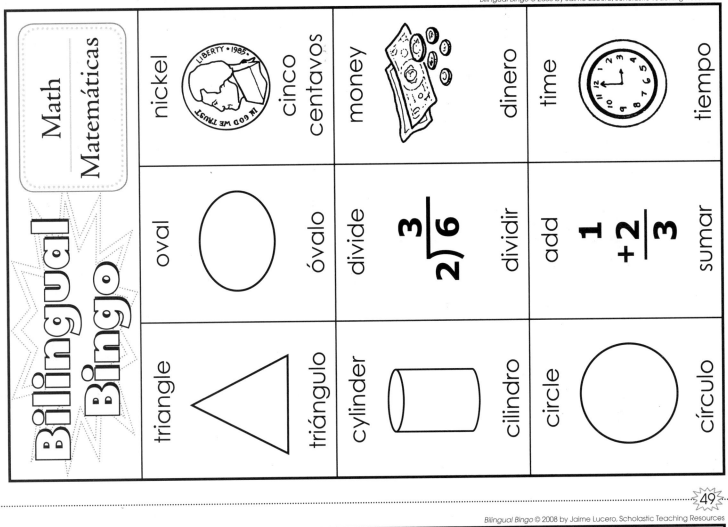

nickel — cinco centavos	oval — óvalo	triangle — triángulo
money — dinero	divide — dividir $2\overline{)6}$ with 3	cylinder — cilindro
time — tiempo	add — sumar $\begin{array}{r}1\\+2\\\hline 3\end{array}$	circle — círculo

49

Bilingual Bingo

Math / Matemáticas

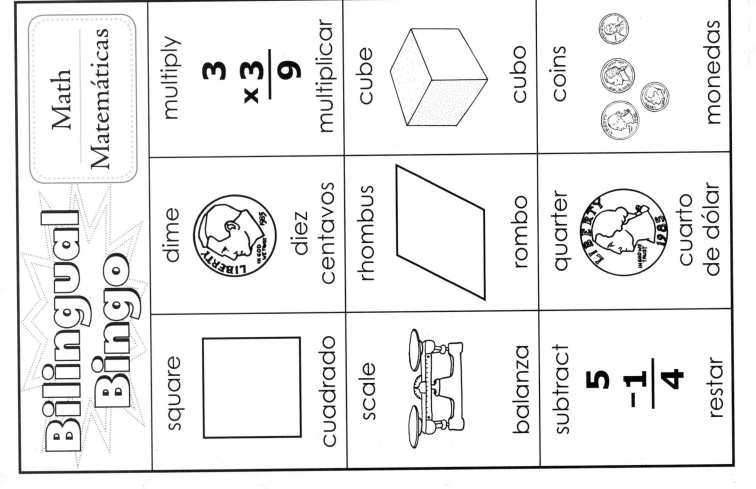

multiply — multiplicar $\begin{array}{r}3\\\times 3\\\hline 9\end{array}$	cube — cubo	coins — monedas
dime — diez centavos	rhombus — rombo	quarter — cuarto de dólar
square — cuadrado	scale — balanza	subtract — restar $\begin{array}{r}5\\-1\\\hline 4\end{array}$

Bilingual Bingo

Math
Matemáticas

circle / círculo	quarter / cuarto de dólar	time / tiempo
rhombus / rombo	oval / óvalo	triangle / triángulo
dime / diez centavos	cube / cubo	coins / monedas

Bilingual Bingo

Math
Matemáticas

subtract / restar $\begin{array}{r} 5 \\ -1 \\ \hline 4 \end{array}$	rectangle / rectángulo	add / sumar $\begin{array}{r} 1 \\ +2 \\ \hline 3 \end{array}$
nickel / cinco centavos	penny / centavo	cylinder / cilindro
square / cuadrado	divide / dividir $3\,)\overline{6}$	scale / balanza

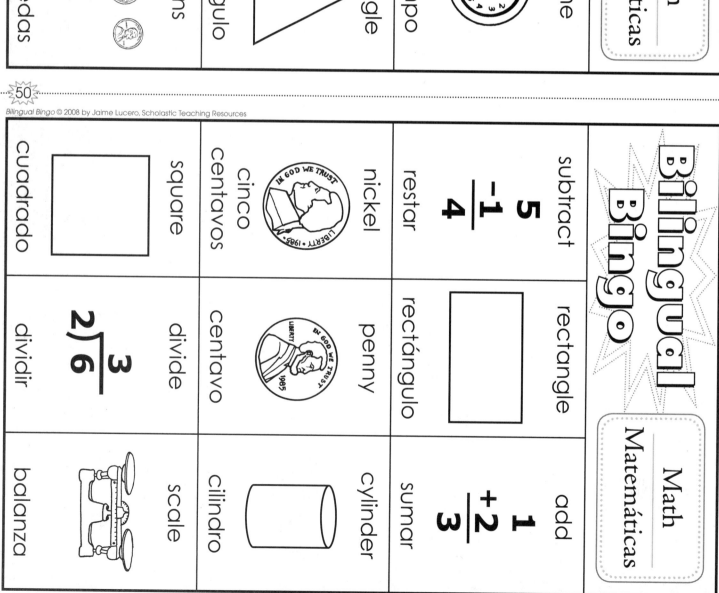

lips	foot	hand	chin
labios	pie	mano	barbilla
mouth	ears	neck	ankle
boca	oídos	cuello	tobillo
arms	palm	nose	wrist
brazos	palma	nariz	muñeca
head	hair	fingers	eyelash
cabeza	cabello	dedos	pestaña
eye	eyebrow	knee	elbow
ojo	ceja	rodilla	codo

Bilingual Bingo

My Body
Mi Cuerpo

ears / oídos 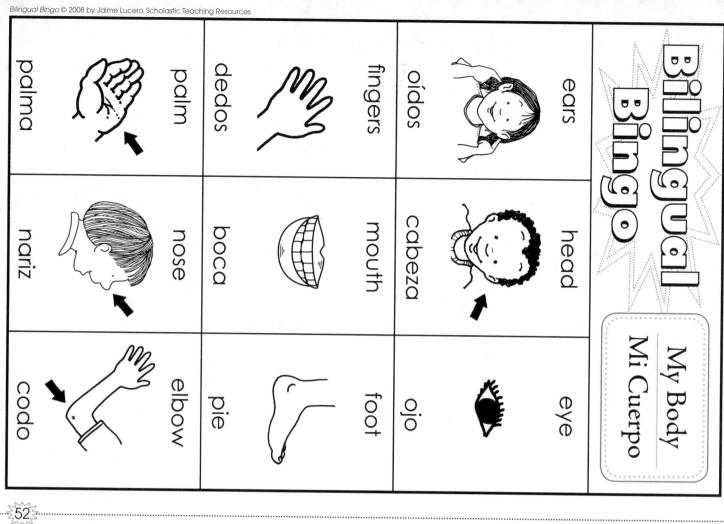	head / cabeza	eye / ojo
fingers / dedos	mouth / boca	foot / pie
palm / palma	nose / nariz	elbow / codo

Bilingual Bingo

My Body
Mi Cuerpo

lips / labios	knee / rodilla	arms / brazos
hair / cabello	wrist / muñeca	neck / cuello
eyelash / pestaña	chin / barbilla	ankle / tobillo

Bilingual Bingo

My Body / Mi Cuerpo

wrist / muñeca	eye / ojo	hair / cabello
eyebrow / ceja	fingers / dedos	hand / mano
neck / cuello	ankle / tobillo	nose / nariz

Bilingual Bingo

My Body / Mi Cuerpo

arms / brazos	knee / rodilla	chin / barbilla
foot / pie	lips / labios	elbow / codo
palm / palma	ears / oídos	eyelash / pestaña

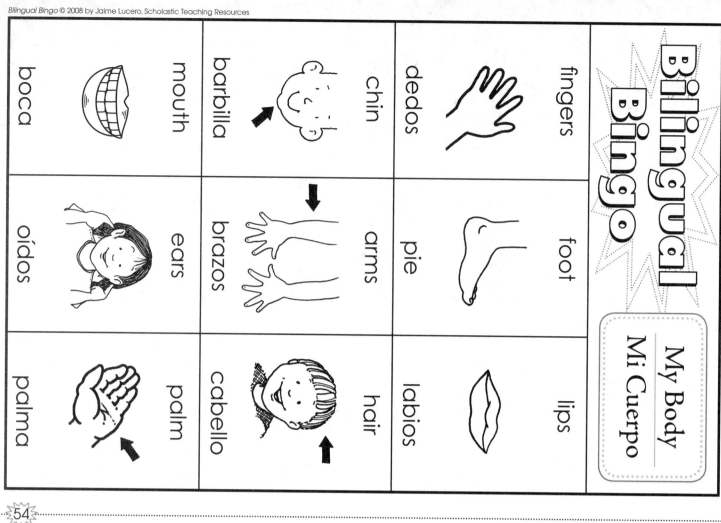

Bilingual Bingo

My Body / Mi Cuerpo

fingers	foot	lips
dedos	pie	labios
chin	arms	hair
barbilla	brazos	cabello
mouth	ears	palm
boca	oídos	palma

Bilingual Bingo

My Body / Mi Cuerpo

eye	knee	head
ojo	rodilla	cabeza
hand	neck	elbow
mano	cuello	codo
nose	eyebrow	wrist
nariz	ceja	muñeca

Bilingual Bingo

My Body / Mi Cuerpo

wrist / muñeca	neck / cuello	ears / oídos
ankle / tobillo	elbow / codo	fingers / dedos
eye / ojo	nose / nariz	eyelash / pestaña

Bilingual Bingo

My Body / Mi Cuerpo

mouth / boca	lips / labios	foot / pie
eyebrow / ceja	hair / cabello	hand / mano
knee / rodilla	head / cabeza	chin / barbilla

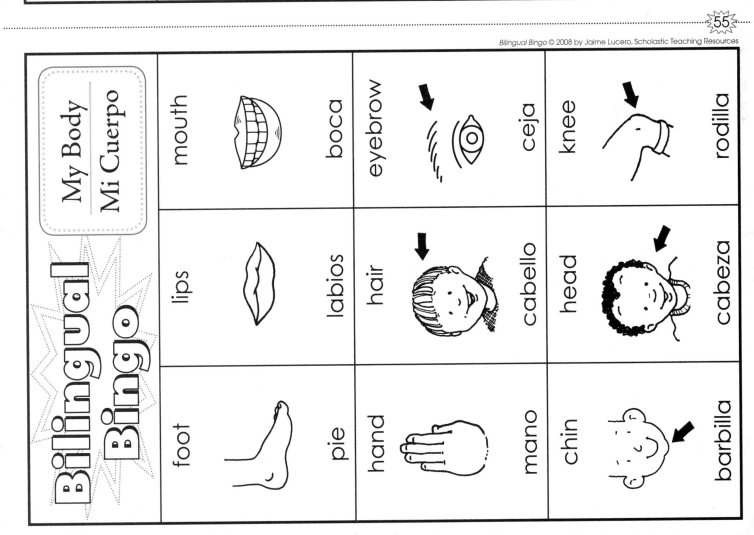

Numbers • Números

zero	one	two	three
0	1	2	3
cero	uno	dos	tres

four	five	six	seven
4	5	6	7
cuatro	cinco	seis	siete

eight	nine	ten	eleven
8	9	10	11
ocho	nueve	diez	once

twelve	thirteen	fourteen	fifteen
12	13	14	15
doce	trece	catorce	quince

twenty	fifty	one hundred	one thousand
20	50	100	1,000
veinte	cincuenta	cien	mil

Bilingual Bingo

Numbers / Números

twelve **12** doce	eight **8** ocho	two **2** dos
zero **0** cero	three **3** tres	ten **10** diez
eleven **11** once	seven **7** siete	five **5** cinco

Bilingual Bingo

Numbers / Números

six **6** seis	fifty **50** cincuenta	four **4** cuatro
one **1** uno	one thousand **1,000** mil	thirteen **13** trece
nine **9** nueve	one hundred **100** cien	twenty **20** veinte

Bilingual Bingo

Numbers
Números

five	fourteen	one
5	14	1
cinco	catorce	uno
thirteen	eight	nine
13	8	9
trece	ocho	nueve
seven	ten	twenty
7	10	20
siete	diez	veinte

Bilingual Bingo

Numbers
Números

two	fifteen	three
2	15	3
dos	quince	tres
one thousand	zero	fifty
1,000	0	50
mil	cero	cincuenta
twelve	six	eleven
12	6	11
doce	seis	once

Bilingual Bingo

Numbers / Números

one hundred **100** cien	twelve **12** doce	fifteen **15** quince
five **5** cinco	one **1** uno	two **2** dos
zero **0** cero	twenty **20** veinte	ten **10** diez

Bilingual Bingo

Numbers / Números

three **3** tres	six **6** seis	fourteen **14** catorce
eight **8** ocho	seven **7** siete	nine **9** nueve
fifty **50** cincuenta	four **4** cuatro	thirteen **13** trece

Bilingual Bingo

Numbers / Números

fifty	50	cincuenta
fifteen	15	quince
eleven	11	once
five	5	cinco
two	2	dos
zero	0	cero
three	3	tres
fourteen	14	catorce
ten	10	diez

Bilingual Bingo

Numbers / Números

nine	9	nueve
one thousand	1,000	mil
thirteen	13	trece
twelve	12	doce
eight	8	ocho
one	1	uno
six	6	seis
one hundred	100	cien
four	4	cuatro

marker	backpack	slide	eraser
marcador	mochila	resbalón	borrador
glue	pencil	globe	book
pegamento	lápiz	esfera terrestre	libro
ruler	bookcase	chalkboard	clock
regla	estante para libros	pizarra	reloj
crayon	desk	lunch box	notepad
crayón	escritorio	caja del almuerzo	libreta
paint	pencil sharpener	scissors	flag
pintura	sacapuntas	tijeras	bandera

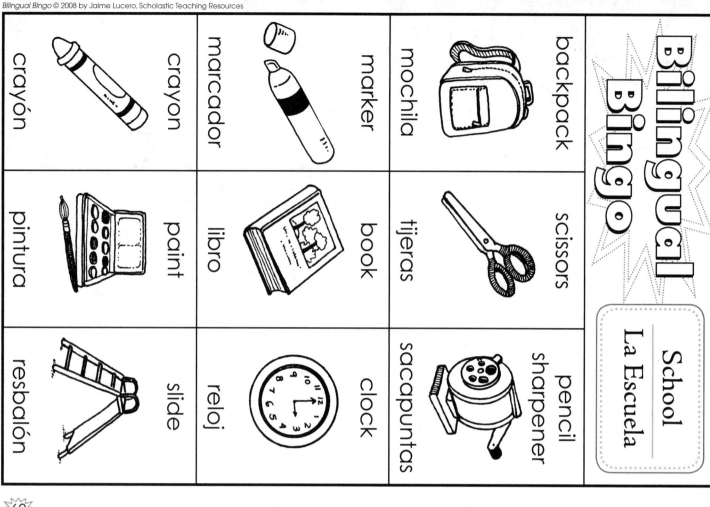

Bilingual Bingo

School
La Escuela

backpack / mochila	scissors / tijeras	pencil sharpener / sacapuntas
marker / marcador	book / libro	clock / reloj
crayon / crayon / crayón	paint / pintura	slide / resbalón

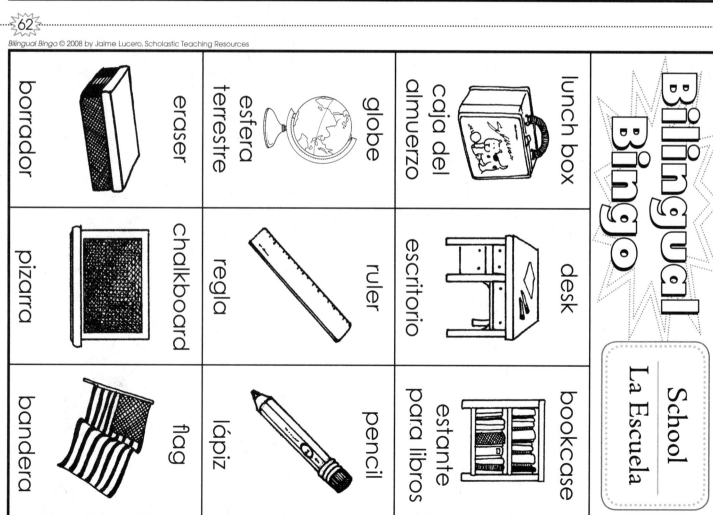

Bilingual Bingo

School
La Escuela

lunch box / caja del almuerzo	desk / escritorio	bookcase / estante para libros
globe / esfera terrestre	ruler / regla	pencil / lápiz
eraser / borrador	chalkboard / pizarra	flag / bandera

Bilingual Bingo

School / La Escuela

clock / reloj 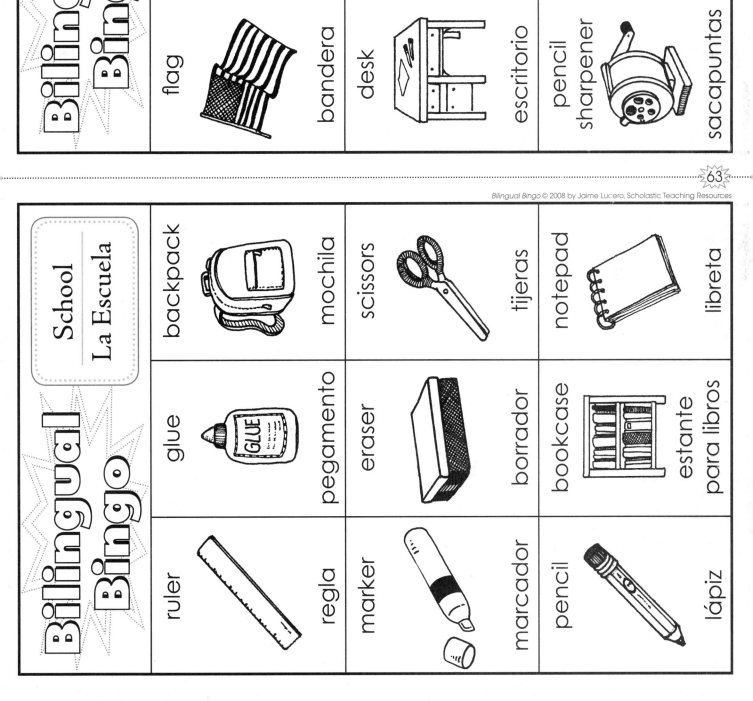	book / libro	globe / esfera terrestre
lunch box / caja del almuerzo	slide / resbalón	chalkboard / pizarra
flag / bandera	desk / escritorio	pencil sharpener / sacapuntas

Bilingual Bingo

School / La Escuela

backpack / mochila	scissors / tijeras	notepad / libreta
glue / pegamento	eraser / borrador	bookcase / estante para libros
ruler / regla	marker / marcador	pencil / lápiz

Bilingual Bingo

School
La Escuela

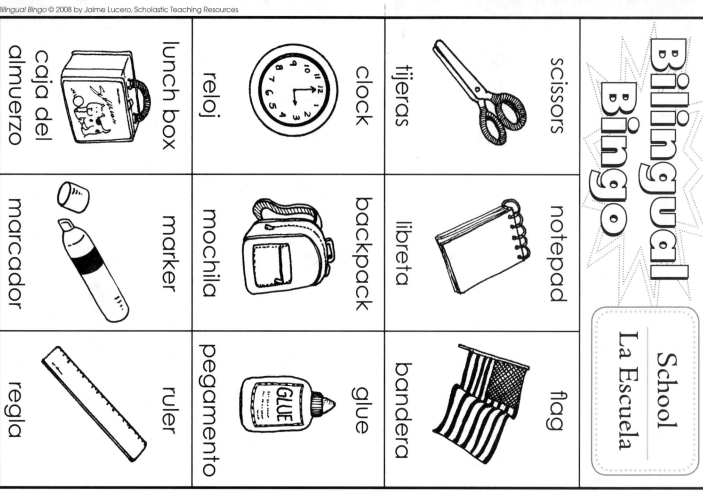

scissors tijeras	notepad libreta	flag bandera
clock reloj	backpack mochila	glue pegamento
lunch box caja del almuerzo	marker marcador	ruler regla

Bilingual Bingo

School
La Escuela

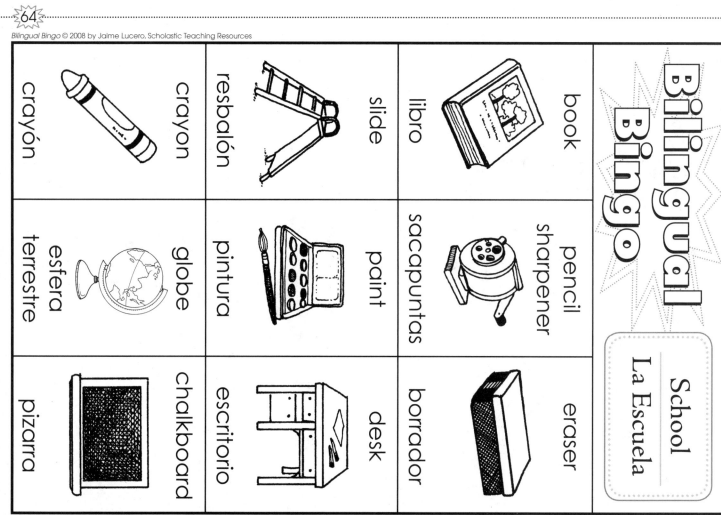

book libro	pencil sharpener sacapuntas	eraser borrador
slide resbalón	paint pintura	desk escritorio
crayon crayón	globe esfera terrestre	chalkboard pizarra

Bilingual Bingo

School
La Escuela

eraser / borrador	book / libro	paint / pintura
bookcase / estante para libros	ruler / regla	marker / marcador
chalkboard / pizarra	backpack / mochila	clock / reloj

Bilingual Bingo

School
La Escuela

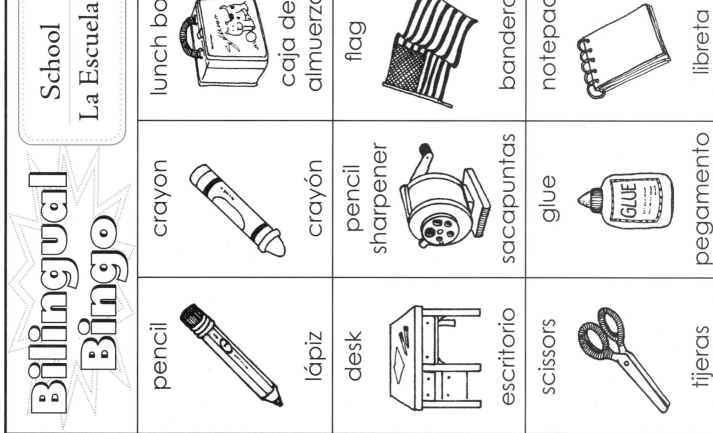

lunch box / caja del almuerzo	crayon / crayón	pencil / lápiz
flag / bandera	pencil sharpener / sacapuntas	desk / escritorio
notepad / libreta	glue / pegamento	scissors / tijeras

Science • La Ciencia

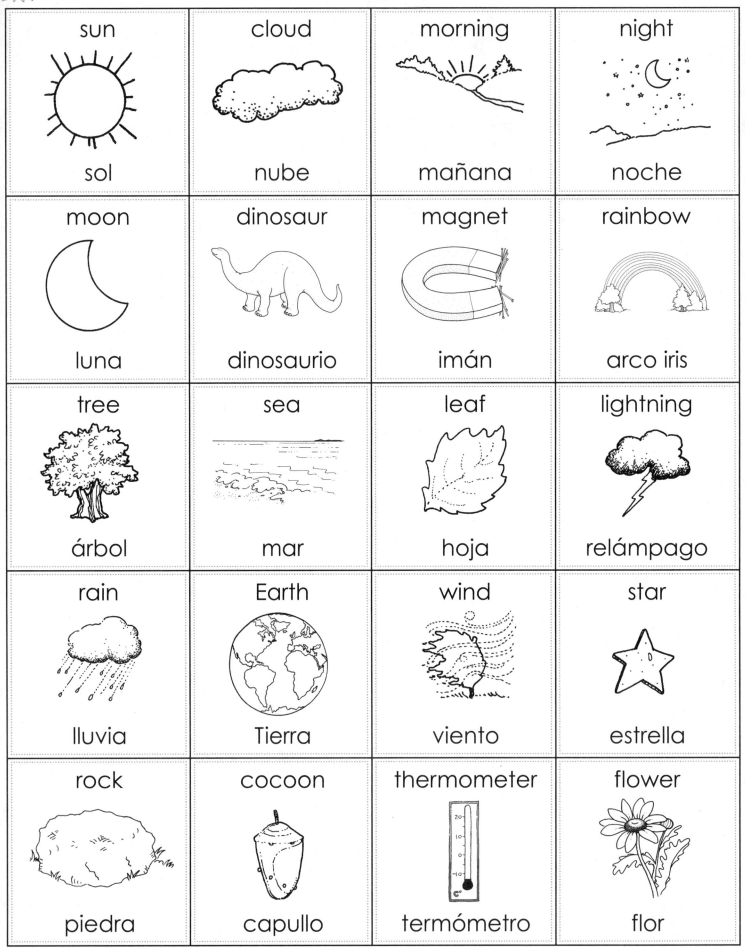

sun	cloud	morning	night
sol	nube	mañana	noche
moon	dinosaur	magnet	rainbow
luna	dinosaurio	imán	arco iris
tree	sea	leaf	lightning
árbol	mar	hoja	relámpago
rain	Earth	wind	star
lluvia	Tierra	viento	estrella
rock	cocoon	thermometer	flower
piedra	capullo	termómetro	flor

Bilingual Bingo

Science / La Ciencia		
sun / sol	star / estrella	lightning / relámpago
tree / árbol	night / noche	dinosaur / dinosaurio
rain / lluvia	morning / mañana	wind / viento

Bilingual Bingo

Science / La Ciencia		
moon / luna	sea / mar	magnet / imán
rainbow / arco iris	Earth / Tierra	cocoon / capullo
flower / flor	cloud / nube	rock / piedra

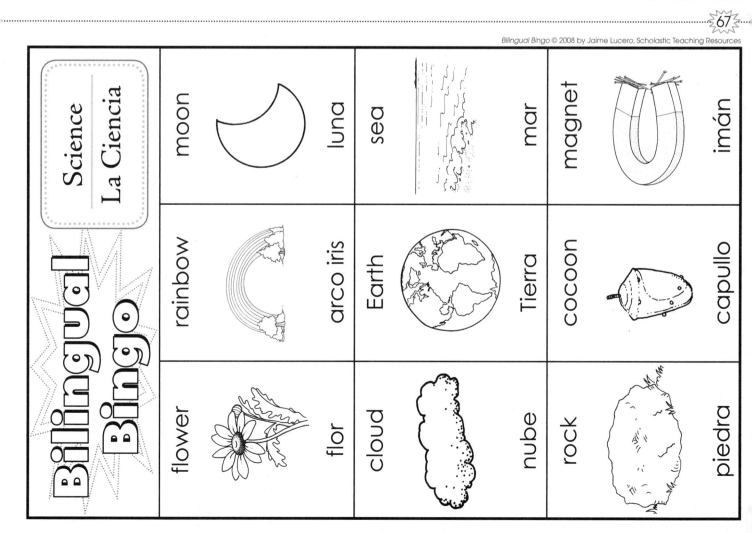

Bilingual Bingo

Science
La Ciencia

Earth	lightning	magnet
Tierra	relámpago	imán
night	flower	rain
noche	flor	lluvia
thermometer	star	leaf
termómetro	estrella	hoja

Bilingual Bingo

Science
La Ciencia

wind	cocoon	morning
viento	capullo	mañana
rainbow	moon	sea
arco iris	luna	mar
tree	rock	sun
árbol	piedra	sol

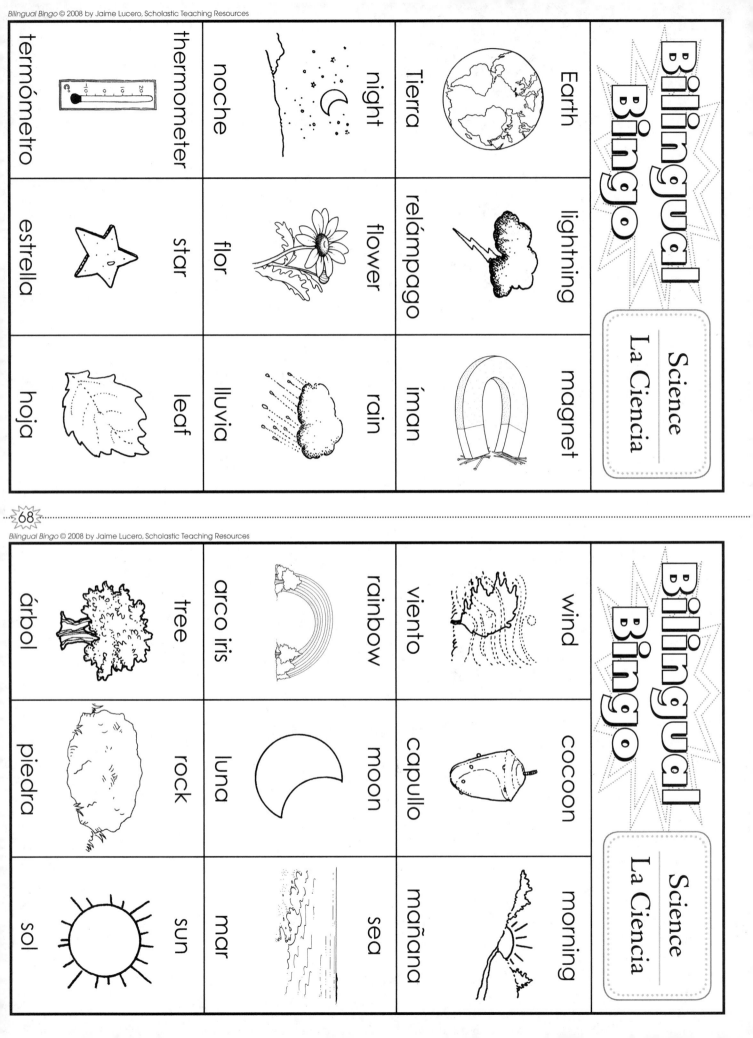

Bilingual Bingo

Science / La Ciencia

Earth / Tierra	star / estrella	morning / mañana
thermometer / termómetro	night / noche	dinosaur / dinosaurio
leaf / hoja	lightning / relámpago	rain / lluvia

Bilingual Bingo

Science / La Ciencia

tree / árbol	sea / mar	moon / luna
sun / sol	wind / viento	magnet / imán
rainbow / arco iris	cloud / nube	flower / flor

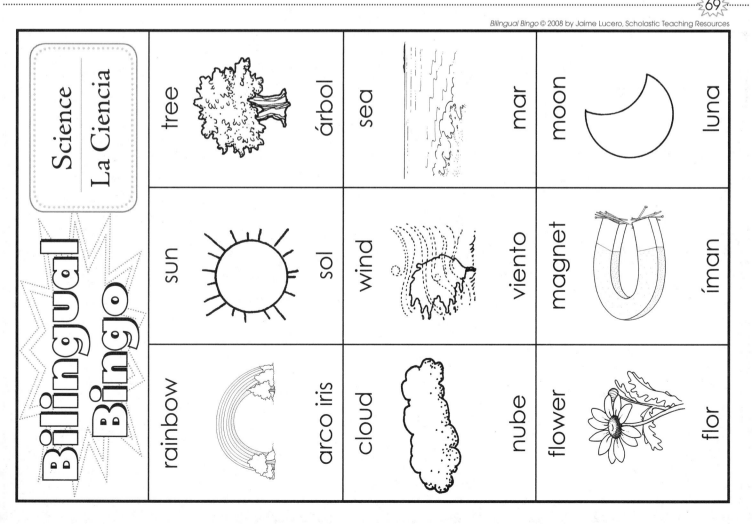

Bilingual Bingo

Science
La Ciencia

cloud	dinosaur	sea
nube	dinosaurio	mar
leaf	wind	thermometer
hoja	viento	termómetro
moon	cocoon	Earth
luna	capullo	Tierra

Bilingual Bingo

Science
La Ciencia

rain	rainbow	magnet
lluvia	arco iris	imán
sun	tree	morning
sol	árbol	mañana
rock	flower	lightning
piedra	flor	relámpago

Transportation • Transportación

train	car	bicycle	skateboard
tren	automóvil	bicicleta	monopatín
airplane	horse	bus	sled
avión	caballo	autobús	trineo
spaceship	ship	truck	hot-air balloon
nave espacial	barco	camión	globo aerostático
motorcycle	ice skates	school bus	canoe
motocicleta	patines de hielo	autobús escolar	canoa
taxi	fire truck	helicopter	wagon
taxi	camión de bomberos	helicóptero	carreta

Bilingual Bingo © 2008 by Jaime Lucero, Scholastic Teaching Resources

Bilingual Bingo

Transportation
Transportación

train	airplane	car
tren	avión	automóvil
motorcycle	spaceship	firetruck
motocicleta	nave espacial	camión de bomberos
taxi	ice skates	ship
taxi	patines de hielo	barco

Bilingual Bingo © 2008 by Jaime Lucero, Scholastic Teaching Resources

Bilingual Bingo

Transportation
Transportación

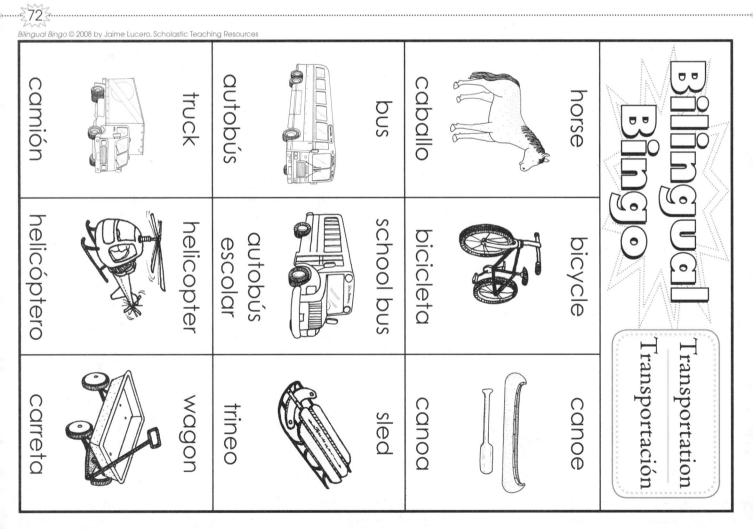

horse	bus	truck
caballo	autobús	camión
bicycle	school bus	helicopter
bicicleta	autobús escolar	helicóptero
canoe	sled	wagon
canoa	trineo	carreta

Bilingual Bingo

Transportation / Transportación

airplane / avión	helicopter / helicóptero	spaceship / nave espacial
taxi / taxi	train / tren	wagon / carreta
horse / caballo	ship / barco	motorcycle / motocicleta

Transportation / Transportación

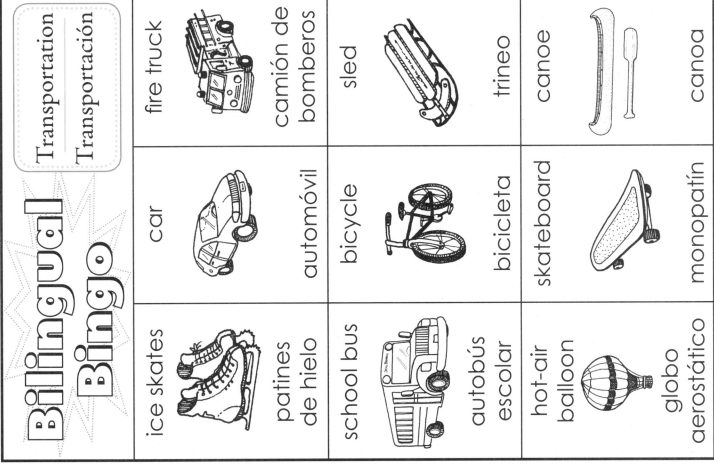

fire truck / camión de bomberos	sled / trineo	canoe / canoa
car / automóvil	bicycle / bicicleta	skateboard / monopatín
ice skates / patines de hielo	school bus / autobús escolar	hot-air balloon / globo aerostático

Bilingual Bingo

Transportation
Transportación

airplane / avión	wagon / carreta	train / tren
sled / trineo	taxi / taxi	fire truck / camión de bomberos
canoe / canoa	motorcycle / motocicleta	bicycle / bicicleta

Bilingual Bingo

Transportation
Transportación

skateboard / monopatín	hot-air balloon / globo aerostático	horse / caballo
ice skates / patines de hielo	truck / camión	helicopter / helicóptero
car / automóvil	bus / autobús	spaceship / nave espacial

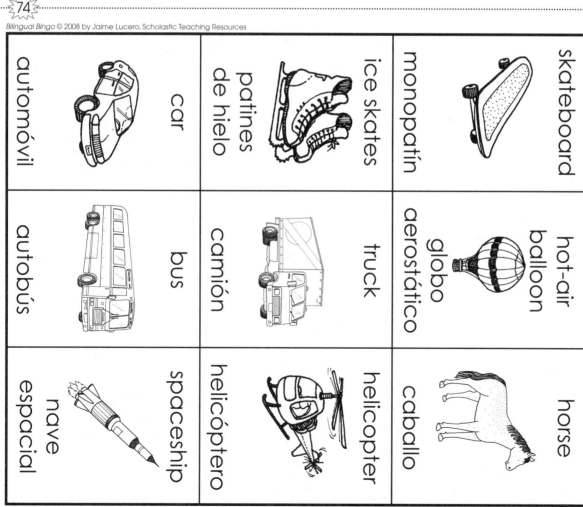
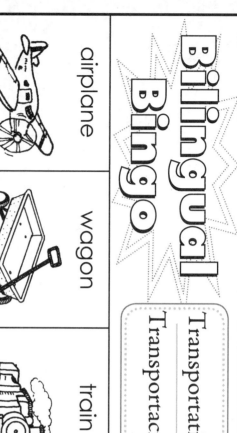

Bilingual Bingo

Transportation
Transportación

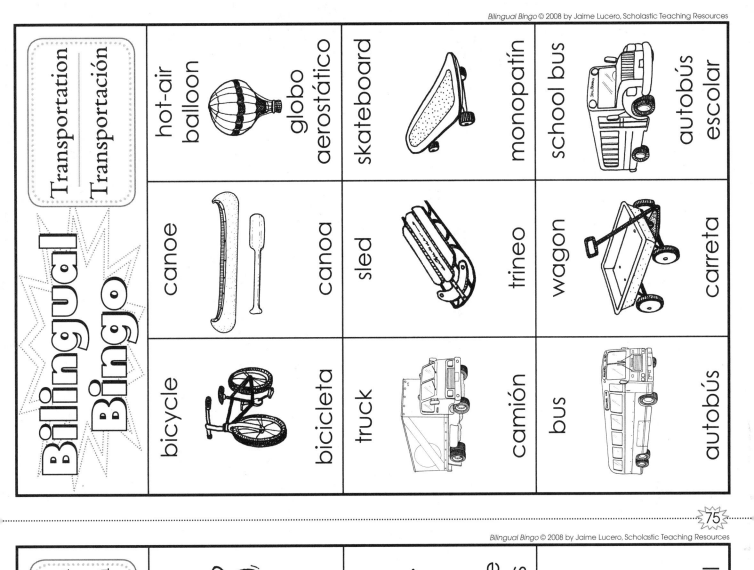

hot-air balloon	skateboard	school bus
globo aerostático	monopatín	autobús escolar
canoe	sled	wagon
canoa	trineo	carreta
bicycle	truck	bus
bicicleta	camión	autobús

Bilingual Bingo

Transportation
Transportación

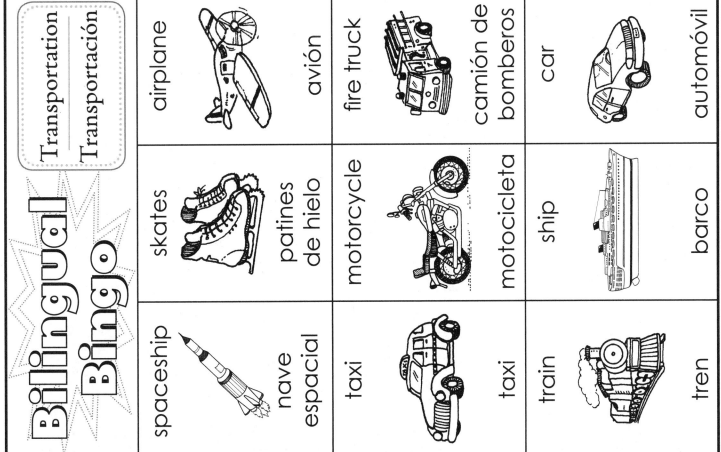

airplane	fire truck	car
avión	camión de bomberos	automóvil
skates	motorcycle	ship
patines de hielo	motocicleta	barco
spaceship	taxi	train
nave espacial	taxi	tren

The Zoo • El Zoológico

polar bear	penguin	bat	tiger
oso polar	pingüino	murciélago	tigre
hippopotamus	snake	zebra	crocodile
hipopótamo	serpiente	cebra	cocodrilo
lion	monkey	elephant	parrot
león	mono	elefante	papagayo
walrus	shark	eel	seal
morsa	tiburón	anguila	foca
iguana	gorilla	porcupine	ostrich
iguana	gorila	puerco espín	avestruz

Bilingual Bingo

The Zoo
El Zoológico

lion león	hippopotamus hipopótamo	porcupine puerco espín
shark tiburón	gorilla gorila	iguana iguana
snake serpiente	ostrich avestruz	seal foca

Bilingual Bingo

The Zoo
El Zoológico

parrot papagayo	zebra cebra	walrus morsa
crocodile cocodrilo	elephant elefante	eel anguila
tiger tigre	monkey mono	bat murciélago

Bilingual Bingo

The Zoo
El Zoológico

shark / tiburón	lion / león	iguana / iguana
penguin / pingüino	gorilla / gorila	eel / anguila
ostrich / avestruz	polar bear / oso polar	crocodile / cocodrilo

Bilingual Bingo

The Zoo
El Zoológico

porcupine / puerco espín	seal / foca	snake / serpiente
elephant / elefante	zebra / cebra	monkey / mono
parrot / papagayo	tiger / tigre	bat / murciélago

Bilingual Bingo

The Zoo / El Zoológico

gorilla / gorila	tiger / tigre	hippopotamus / hipopótamo
porcupine / puerco espín	parrot / papagayo	zebra / cebra
lion / león	penguin / pingüino	iguana / iguana

Bilingual Bingo

The Zoo / El Zoológico

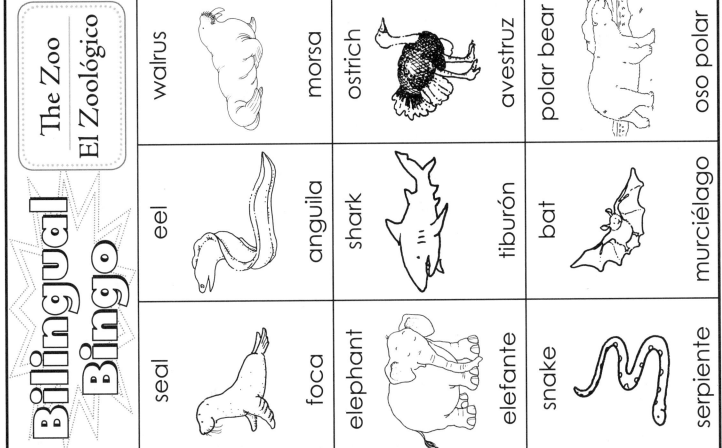

walrus / morsa	ostrich / avestruz	polar bear / oso polar
eel / anguila	shark / tiburón	bat / murciélago
seal / foca	elephant / elefante	snake / serpiente

Bilingual Bingo

The Zoo
El Zoológico

ostrich avestruz 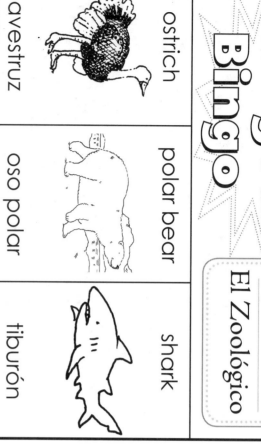	polar bear oso polar	shark tiburón
lion león	porcupine puerco espín	monkey mono
crocodile cocodrilo	penguin pingüino	iguana iguana

Bilingual Bingo

The Zoo
El Zoológico

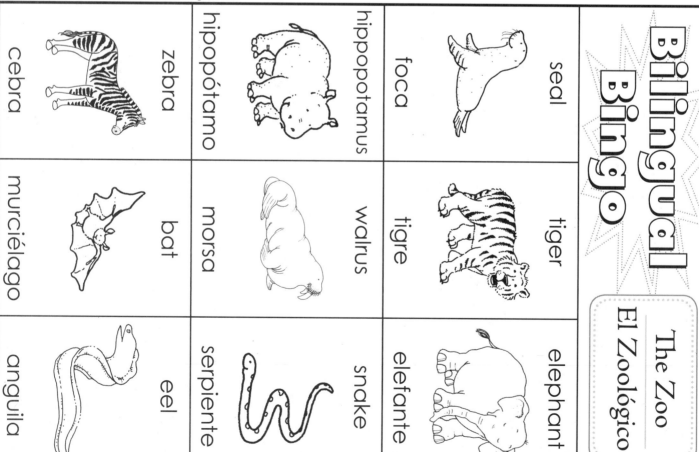

seal foca	tiger tigre	elephant elefante
hippopotamus hipopótamo	walrus morsa	snake serpiente
zebra cebra	bat murciélago	eel anguila